The Practice of Political Spirituality:

Episodes from the Public Career of Abraham Kuyper, 1879-1918

The Practice of
Political Spirituality:

*Episodes from the Public Career
of Abraham Kuyper, 1879-1918*

by McKendree R. Langley

PAIDEIA PRESS
Jordan Station, Ontario, Canada

Canadian Cataloguing in Publication Data

Langley, McKendree R.
    The Practice of Political Spirituality

Includes bibliographical references
ISBN 0-88815-070-9

1. Kuyper, Abraham, 1837-1920.
2. Statesmen — Netherlands — Biography.
3. Theologians — Netherlands — Biography.
I. Title.

DJ283.K89L3 1984   949.2'06'0924   C84-098884-2

Cover design by Rachelle Longtin.

ISBN 0-88815-070-9
Printed in Canada.

Contents

Preface

*I*n *The Practice of Political Spirituality* McKendree Langley has provided us with a significant little volume, simply written and very readable, about a subject which ought certainly to be at the heart of every Christian's interest today. Battles which go much deeper than the legal ones are being waged these days with regard to the separation of Church and State. As institutions, these may well be separate; statecraft (political activity) and spirituality (this in its biblical sense) *can*not be. But today there is also the opposite threat of a Christianity that has become so politicized that the dynamic Good News of God, viz. our liberation from the power, guilt and penalty of sin and restoration to a life of fellowship with God and our neighbor, becomes obscured. Is there a third route possible, between the Scylla of other-worldliness and the Charybdis of a politicized Christianity? There is, as Prof. Langley's book clearly shows—the way of political spirituality.

For this reason Langley's book is extremely timely, providing a perspective that is badly needed but often missing from current American discussions. In it the author, of a Presbyterian and Anglo-Saxon background, reflects on what he felicitously calls the political spirituality of Abraham Kuyper. Kuyper, a prominent representative of the movement for the biblical renewal of life in

The Netherlands in the last decades of the previous century and right up to the end of the First World War, is still too little known in American evangelical circles, but he was without any doubt one of the most important Christian thinkers and leaders of the modern period. He lived through times which, as to fundamental religious directions, were very much like our own, times of increasingly revolutionary rejection of the sovereign God and His revealed will, on the one hand, and, on the other, of a notable evangelical re-awakening and an increasing awareness, on the part of evangelical Christians, of their collective vocation to engage more actively (with spiritual weapons, of course) in the great Battle of spirits which has always, even when not sufficiently recognized, been the root driving force of human history.

That Battle, in Kuyper's day as now, involved, in the first instance, the struggle of Christian parents to reclaim from the so-called religiously neutral and all-too-sovereign State their own God-given authority (thus, their right) to educate their children in all subjects and at all levels of instruction in accordance with the revealed will of God, and thus simultaneously to challenge the State's authority to determine the meaning or direction of life. Classical liberalism (from which our American conservatives and liberals both derive) did not, in this respect, differ from present-day totalitarian states.

In our own day, therefore, Langley's book should prove eminently useful to all Christians who confess, on the basis of the Scriptures of the Old and New Testaments received as the authoritative Word of the living God, that the risen and ascended Christ is Lord, that He sits at the Father's right hand, possessing and exercising all authority both in heaven and on earth (Matthew 28:18; I Peter 3:22). Prof. Langley expresses the hope "that as believers in various countries and situations consider their own attitudes toward society, they will examine the legacy of political spirituality left by Abraham Kuyper, a legacy which provides not the final word on Christian political action, but a basis for reflection and discussion" (p. 160).

"Political spirituality"—there is a notion evangelical Christians are going increasingly to have to ponder in a more serious and sustained manner in the coming days, and Langley's book is an excellent place to start. He describes it as "an integrated Christian attitude" that provides "the ability to discern the directions sin and grace take in public affairs,"[1] and distinguishes it from political tactics. "Tactics change as times and situations differ, 'political spirituality' remains part of a Christian's obligation to do all things to the glory of God." (p. 3). Langley, who is an historian, not a philosopher or systematic theologian, does not attempt to analyze in any systematic way the meaning-content of the concept. What he offers us instead is an examination of the remarkable political career of Abraham Kuyper as an illustration of the practice of political spirituality. The book is not a biography of Kuyper either;[2] rather, it describes important episodes in his life which serve to demonstrate concretely Kuyper's political spirituality.

In America, Kuyper, where he is known at all, has been known almost exclusively as a theologian and devotionalist.[3] In itself that reputation is, of course, well deserved; what it fails to do is to focus our attention on what was preeminently great and of unusual historical significance in Kuyper, or that which makes him an outstandingly important figure for Christians of our generation and of others yet to come, in all parts of the world. That was, without doubt, his richly informed perception that the secular humanism which, after the French and subsequent revolutions, was breaking out everywhere and assuming a position of dominance in government and cultural circles was an integral and comprehensive view of man and the world totally opposed in its direction to the Christian one, and that the ensuing situation in western societies required a new, more active and more organized Christian stance in return.

But it was also the huge successes he reaped in this

venture. God had placed just this man on the scene at just the right moment, and through his extensive journalistic and educational enterprises, and particularly his strenuous political activities (where he finally succeeded in breaking the stranglehold of Liberalism's long-held hegemony in his nation's political life — not, by the way, in the interest of conservatism — and rose to become Prime Minister), he aroused a large body of Christians to engage in the Struggle, beginning, as we said earlier, with their assuming their rightful *parental* responsibility for the religious direction of their children's education and, at the same time, with their entering the contest, as a body of Christians organized on an accepted political program of principles, for the political direction of the life of the State.

The Battle *had* to assume this political aspect, because the rise of the modern socialist/communist movement had lifted up the idol of the Socialist Redeemer State, a totalitarian State which forcibly (by law or by arms or both) controls all of society and thus must eliminate the various social spheres which properly are free of state control. This is what the current struggle in Poland is all about, but, closer to home, the same battle is waged by law and in the courts. If in Poland it is the question of the right to exist of a labor union like *Solidarity*, free of State-domination, closer to home it is the question of the rights of parents in the institution of the family and of other non-public associations and institutions, of all those other spheres which do not owe their existence to the State and so must be allowed to fulfill their calling in the creation.

Kuyper was simply building, as Prof. Langley points out "on the perspective inherited from Calvin's sixteenth century *Institutes of the Christian Religion* and even from Augustine's fifth century *City of God*. Augustine and Calvin made important statements about the comprehensive character of the kingdom of God and the task of believers in hostile pagan and apostate environments.

Kuyper provided an updated version of this comprehensive Christian vision in our modern age of indifferent secularism"[4] (pp. 163-164).

That is the importance of Kuyper for us today. The episodes Langley describes out of his long career of distinguished service to Christ the King were great and exciting moments in the history of Christ's people on earth, and we American Christians should know a good deal more about them than we do now. There is much for us to learn, and more to think about, in all those years of experience of our fellow-Christians who already more than a century ago were becoming aware of the new situation in the world which continuing critical events throughout the world are now forcing upon our attention.

Moreover, we American Christians, like Americans generally, have been inclined to view our struggle as engaging one particular issue at a time, and we are only now just beginning to be aware, as Kuyper was in his time, of the *systematic denial*, in our society, our schools and universities, *of the living God who has revealed Himself in Jesus Christ*. Consequently, we are only at the starting-point of considering how responsibly and effectively to bring a *corporate* and *integrated* Christian witness to bear on that situation. Prof. Langley's book should be of help to us here by showing us that a piecemeal, one-issue-at-a-time approach is not so much a valuable national characteristic as it is a lack of sensitive, biblically inspired vision as to our Christian political — and cultural — calling in today's world.

Of course, there may be evangelical Christians in the United States — and elsewhere — who are still uncertain about, or even ignorant of, the comprehensiveness of the Struggle that is going on between what Augustine called the City of God and the city of this world. If there are such, they might well turn to the magazine *The Humanist* in its January/February issue of 1983 (Vol. 43, No. 1) and read the article by John Dunphy, "A Religion for a New

Age" on pp. 23-26, the conclusion of which I quote here. "I am convinced," Dunphy writes, "that the battle for humankind's future must be waged and won in the public school classroom by teachers who correctly perceive their role as the proselytizers of a new faith: a religion of humanity that recognizes and respects the spark of what theologians call divinity in every human being. These teachers . . . will be ministers of another sort, utilizing a classroom instead of a pulpit *to convey humanist values in whatever subject they teach, regardless of the educational level—preschool day care or large state university.* The classroom must and will become an arena of conflict be-tween the old and the new — the rotting corpse of Chris-tianity, together with all its adjacent evils and misery, and the new faith of humanism, resplendent in its promise of a world in which the never-realized Christian ideal of 'love thy neighbor' will finally be achieved" [emphasis mine, H.E.R.]. What, may I ask, is the difference between that and the religious mind-set of the communist rulers of the Soviet Union and the subjugated eastern European bloc of nations? Nor should we think that Mr. Dunphy is an isolated case. On the contrary, he is *representative* of a broad movement, become increasingly militant, a move-ment of the human spirit (in rebellion against the living God and the authority of His ordinances) that has long been at work in our most prestigious prep schools and universities.[5]

No, the Struggle which Kuyper and the Christians of his day perceived to be present in society is a present reali-ty for us also in our society. The important point is that it is a comprehensive, integral Struggle, proceeding from two opposing views on the world, man, the origin and nature of authority. It is a Battle for which we Christians in America have yet to discover a suitable and effective strategy. About this Battle and the Christian strategy that Kuyper developed in order to cope effectively with it, Langley's book offers us, in chapter after chapter, much rich material for our thoughtful consideration and for future study and discussion.

About the individualistic approach we have generally followed in America Kuyper, who did have some little
experience in political life, wrote:[6] "The influence which
emanates from all these [modern secular] organizations is
thus without exception destructive for our Christian confession. One reasons and acts out of principles which are
absolutely opposed to ours. If now one allows oneself to
enter into such organizations and if one mingles in such
organizations with those who are of a wholly other mind,
then what they think or judge becomes the starting-point
of the decisions that are to be taken, and one supports by
one's membership what one, in conformity with one's
Christian confession, may not support but must combat.
In such anarchistic, socialistic [or liberalistic so-called
neutral] associations a spirit is operative which never can
or may be ours. The leadership in such organizations falls
never to us but always and inflexibly to our opponents.
They carry out their intention, and whoever of us em-
barks with them ends up where they want to land but
where we never may land. Thus *our* principle settles down
at the point of non-activity, loses its position of influence
and is pressed into the corner . . . mingling with these
leaders of another spirit in the organization itself leads
always to a bitterly sad fiasco of the Christian principle
and prepares the way for *their* victory and for *our* over-
throw . . ."

It would appear, judging from the record to date,
that Kuyper wrote those words with a keen understanding
and a broad, biblically grounded cultural sensitivity. The
political spirituality Prof. Langley is addressing in his
book is one way in which this sensitivity finds expression.

It is well to remember, in reading Kuyper's words,
that by "Christian principle" Kuyper is referring to what
has been revealed to us in the Bible about God the
Creator, the Source of all authority in the creation, the
divine ordinances for the creation, the religious nature of
man and his covenant relation to God, etc., while over

against that he sees, as common to all the modern movements (though to differing degrees of consistency), the source of all authority and law in man himself, who is autonomous, (i.e., not responsible to Anyone beyond himself or the world of which he is a part). In other words, in present-day language, Kuyper is referring to the constant Struggle that goes on for control of God's creation between the people of God (who may do wrong) and the forces of secular humanism in its various forms (which are influenced in mysterious ways to do good by God's creation revelation and His restraining grace).

Those who fear that theocratic repression must be the result of any Christian group's obtaining governmental power—and that *is* a widespread fear (in large part due to the medieval legacy)—will most certainly want to familiarize themselves with Kuyper's views, and with what he persistently strove for and actually accomplished. Once again he appears as a monumental figure in the history of the Christian movement. For Kuyper fought to achieve tolerance and an acceptance of public pluralism in modern society. On this most critical point too Langley's book is instructive. Kuyper, he shows, was not interested in excluding liberals or socialists from the government, to the extent that they really represented a segment of the Dutch electorate (the principle of proportional representation, as opposed to the American practice of winner take all[7]). As a matter of fact, Kuyper wished to secure and protect their *legitimate* rights, as opposed to the illegitimate monolithic hegemony the Liberals had long been enjoying. What he sought was *equal* acceptance for those citizens who wished to participate in government on the basis of their Christian convictions, something the Liberals' inflexible intolerance had worked to prevent.[8]

Prof. Langley's brief summaries or comments at the close of each chapter are always helpful, and on the point we have just been discussing he gives us a most important consideration to reflect upon when he writes: "Kuyper's assumption of power was an example of the paradox of partisanship. Assuming a partisan position and accepting the partisanships of others can open the way for public impartiality. Mutual respect for differences in a pluralist framework can make realities of governmental cooperation, mutual respect and the creation of a climate of trust and political stability" (p. 78).

In the past when a book appeared having to do with Abraham Kuyper, it was quite generally assumed, I think, that the book was for a very restricted circle of readers—either Reformed theologians and pastors, particularly those of a Dutch stripe, or persons interested in Dutch ecclesiastical or national history. In these introductory remarks I have tried to place Kuyper where he belongs, at the very center of the history of Christ's people in our modern society where the Struggle constantly becomes more comprehensive and more integral. I have tried to show that a familiarity with the life and work of Kuyper at this time is vital to our clarifying to ourselves what our task is in America as evangelical Christians.

There is another reason why all evangelical Christians in America should embrace Kuyper's political spirituality, the theme of Langley's book, as an important chapter in their own history. Most of Kuyper's vision (though he worked it out farther and discovered many ways to apply it) he received from his noble predecessor in the faith, Guillaume (= Willem) Groen van Prinsterer (1801-1876). Groen, educated at the University of Leiden in law and the classics, was converted to evangelical Christianity in early manhood as a result of the Evangelical Awakening (the Réveil), which had its beginnings when the Scot, Robert Haldane (1764-1842), gave Bible studies in the book of *Romans* and conducted prayer meetings to stimulate a much needed spiritual revival among the theological students at the University of Geneva (Calvin's old Academy) in Switzerland. One of those students, Merle d'Aubigné, had been instrumental in the conversion of Groen.[9] The Réveil swept up the

Rhine valley into the Lowlands and Germany, affecting, among others, a number of men in positions of influence in several European countries.

It was Groen, for instance, who in his *Unbelief and Revolution* (1847), an historic book in the history of Christian thought, demonstrated that the deepest cause of the French Revolution, and of the revolutionary spirit abroad in Europe at the time, was the secular humanism of the eighteenth century Enlightenment. It was he who then summoned his fellow-believers to the task of reforming political life on the basis of Christian principles in place of the revolutionary (i.e., unbelieving) principles of the Enlightenment. This aristocrat of the old stamp, now since his conversion a fellow-believer first of all, predicting the drift of Western politics to the left, was the first to call for the formation of a mass (Christian) political party in The Netherlands. He laid the foundations of Holland's oldest formal political party. It was his work and insight that Kuyper developed.

The work of Groen and Kuyper thus developed out of the Evangelical Awakening; in their work we see the awakening of the body of Christians, after centuries of accommodation to the emerging scientistic world-view, to the real threat of secular humanism as a comprehensive, an integrated attack on the Christian faith and the Christian way of life. Their work thus springs from reviving evangelical life. Both Groen and Kuyper wanted to be remembered simply as "Evangeliebelijders" (Gospel Confessors). For this reason Prof. Langley's little book ought to be read by every thougtful evangelical Christian in North America. The book should serve as a bridge-builder between those who call themselves Evangelicals/ Fundamentalists and more specifically Reformed Christians. Against the secular humanist threat in our society and in God's world we have a task that can only be accomplished if we find ways in our society of working closely together as servants of a common Lord.

There is one thing in Langley's discussion of Kuyper

that leaves me somewhat dissatisfied. That is his discussion of grace, common and special, particularly in Chapters 14 and 16 (pp. 142-144, 165), where he speaks of "the realm (domain) of common grace" and "the realm (domain) of special grace." Kuyper's view on this subject has frequently been discussed in this way, and there has been much discussion of what precisely he meant. Men like Van Ruler, Schilder and S.G. DeGraaf (author of the four volume *Promise and Deliverance*, published in an English translation by Paideia Press) have offered criticisms. This is not the place to enter in any detail into the importance of these discussions for Prof. Langley's theme. Nevertheless, this does constitute a matter of supreme importance. I shall make just two brief comments.

First, in perhaps the most important single article on this question—and how fortunate we are to have it in English!—the late Prof. S.U. Zuidema wrote:[10] "In summary I conclude that Kuyper gave Van Ruler [one of the critics] cause for writing what he did. But no less do I conclude that Kuyper more than once should have given Van Ruler pause in writing what he did" (p. 100). He is referring to a statement he made previously: ". . . Van Ruler has not sufficiently, or rather not at all, taken into account the Kuyper who in principle overcomes and removes the polar tension between particular grace and common grace—precisely in his doctrine of particular grace. I am referring to the Kuyper who teaches—as he does in *De Gemeene Gratie* (Common Grace) II, 298—that particular grace . . . in regeneration . . . works a deeply religious reversal of the 'innermost pivot' of our being . . . [and] next asks how this *reversal* of the 'invisibly small yet all-controlling central point' in man can possibly become effective on the *periphery*, that is to say, how a truly Christian life can blossom forth from such a regeneration . . ." "Here," Zuidema adds, "precisely in his doctrine of regeneration and particular grace, Kuyper radically rises above that haunting dilemma brought on

by the polarly dialectical relation which he usually con-
strued between re-creation [i.e., spiritual life in Christ, or
religion — H.E.R.] and creation [i.e., activities in this
world, or culture — H.E.R.]. In another place (p. 95)
Zuidema makes the matter even clearer: ". . . Kuyper
himself had already made this correction; that in fact the
happy hour arrived that he set forth that Christ as the
Mediator of Redemption not only may lay claim to the
central, spiritual core of man, but also is in principle the
new Root of all of created reality and the Head, the new
Head, of the 'human race.' With that, Kuyper had
broken with his own polarly dualistic contrast between
particular grace and common grace. That is why he could
state more forcefully in his writings on *Pro Rege* than in
those on *Gemeene Gratie* that we are in the service of
Christ throughout the entire domain of common grace"
(*Pro Rege* II, 527).

My second comment is that, without ignoring the
important writings of Klaas Schilder and others on the
subject, I wish just now to call attention particularly to
the work of S.G. DeGraaf, especially (for those who can
read Dutch) his important article "Genade en Natuur"
(Grace and Nature), in the volume *Christus en De Wereld*
(Christ and the World) (Kampen: Kok, 1939), pp.
72-113, which deals in a brilliantly stimulating way with
the subject of common grace.[11]

Happily, just at those points where Kuyper's scien-
tific theological formulations were sometimes a bit less
than satisfactory, it was his practical intuitive insights,
nourished on the Scriptures, that directed him to his
political — and more broadly cultural — action. They
even, as we have just seen, enabled him in time to correct
some of his inadequate formulations. And I am glad that
my friend, McKendree Langley, has brought *this* Kuyper
to our attention.

When Prof. Langley asked me to write an Introduction for his book, I joyfully responded; for it was when as
a young man I, like him a Presbyterian and partly Scotch-

Irish, first went to Holland to study theology (a long time ago, in the Fall of 1939, arriving, in fact, on September 1, the day, early in the morning, that the Second World War broke out with Hitler's Stuka bomber attack on Poland) that I discovered, *in the patterns of everyday life there*, the colossal achievement that, in reliance upon God Almighty, had been realized by Groen and Kuyper and the hosts of faithful confessors of the Name who had entrusted themselves to their leadership.

H. Evan Runner

Notes

1. At a number of places throughout his book, Prof. Langley makes the important point that the directions sin and grace take can only be detected against the backdrop of *a revealed creation-order* (which includes creation norms). It is a point made frequently by Kuyper. See, for instance, p. 167, last paragraph.
2. Fortunately, we have in English a good popular biography of Kuyper: Frank VandenBerg, *Abraham Kuyper*, Eerdmans, 1960, now available in paperback from Paideia Press.
3. This, in spite of the fact that the Stone lectures Kuyper gave in the United States (at Princeton Theological Seminary in New Jersey in 1898) had as their main emphasis that Calvinism was a distinct and comprehensive outlook on man and the world, a world-view, one of the chapters being devoted to "Calvinism and Politics." A chief cause of the difficulty, without a doubt, has been the retreat of the body of believers in the course of the modern centuries so that the Christian community became restricted largely to ecclesiastical assemblies and theological institutions. In other words, the people of the living God had become a kind of ghetto sub-culture in a largely rationalistic or naturalistic society. In such a situation Kuyper's message could scarcely be properly absorbed, far less acted upon.
4. I'm not exactly sure what Prof. Langley means by the term "indifferent secularism." I suppose he is referring to the broad masses, whether a part of the believing community or not, which appear so lethargic, even supine, which, under the prevailing this-worldly, hedonistic world-view of Unbelief, seem so often to be without pur-

pose or direction in their lives. On the other hand, since the Enlightenment of the eighteenth century and the French Revolution,
there has been an increasing aggressiveness in a rapidly growing
group of intellectuals committed to the Unbelief of the Left.

5. It is illuminating, for example, to read Michael Straight's recently
published book *After Long Silence* (N.Y.: W.W. Norton, 1983),
which contains many revelations about the brilliant Communist
circles of Cambridge University in the 1930s.

6. *Pro Rege*, III, 190. We are happy that Paideia Press plans to
publish an English translation (somewhat reduced) of the three
volumes of *Pro Rege* (meaning *For King Jesus*) in the very near
future.

7. The idea of proportional representation, which had been supported by Kuyper's party for decades before it was instituted,
"was accepted finally by all parties as a matter of simple justice.
'It was thought that Parliament should present a perfect mirror of
the different groups that composed the nation.' " (Skillen and
Carlson-Thies: see (a) in Note 8. The last sentence is quoted by
them from an article by Hans Daalder, "The Netherlands:
Opposition in a Segmented Society," in *Political Oppositions in
Western Democracies*, ed. Robert A. Dahl (New Haven: Yale
University Press, 1966), p. 207.

8. Some recent very informative literature on matters raised in the
last paragraph:
    (a) James W. Skillen and Stanley W. Carlson-Thies, "Reli-
gion and Political Development in Nineteenth-Century Holland,"
in *Publius: The Journal of Federalism*, Vol. 12, No. 3 (Summer,
1982), pp. 43-64.
    (b) James W. Skillen, "From Covenant of Grace to Tolerant
Public Pluralism: The Dutch Calvinist Contribution." (Paper
presented at the Workshop on Covenant and Politics of the Center
for Study of Federalism, at Temple University, Philadelphia,
1980.)
    (c) James W. Skillen, "Societal Pluralism: Blessing or Curse
for the Public Good," pp. 166-171 in *The Ethical Dimension of
Political Life: Essays in Honor of John H. Hallowell*, ed. Francis
Canavan, Durham, N.C.: Duke University Press, 1983.

9. Because very little is known in America about this great Christian
leader and his landmark labors in reviving the body of believers
and their influence in the national life of The Netherlands, I
should like to call attention to an excellent article about him in
English in the Fall, 1982 issue of *The Westminster Theological
Journal* (Vol. XLIV, No. 2), pp. 205-249. The article, "Guillaume
Groen van Prinsterer and His Conception of History," was written

by a Groen expert, J.L. van Essen, and translated by Herbert Donald Morton.

10. The article, "Common Grace and Christian Action in Abraham Kuyper" appears in a volume of essays by S.U. Zuidema on modern society and contemporary thought entitled *Communication and Confrontation* (Toronto: Wedge Publishing Foundation, 1972), pp. 52-101, but for the present point see particularly pp. 94-101.

11. In June, 1982 a theological master's thesis was submitted at the Free University of Amsterdam in The Netherlands on "Geschiedenis als Verbondsgeschiedenis: een onderzoek naar de visie van Simon Gerrit de Graaf (1889-1955) op de zin der geschiedenis" (History as History of the Covenant: An Investigation into S.G. DeGraaf's View of the Meaning of History). It includes a discussion of DeGraaf's view of common grace.

Abraham Kuyper and the Contemporary Discussion on Faith and Politics

*D*URING RECENT PRESIDENTIAL CAMPAIGNS a new dimension has been added to national politics: "the born-again" phenomenon. A number of recent presidents have declared themselves to be born-again Christians, and television, radio, books, and national magazines have belabored the point. Many citizens have concluded that religion, morality, and politics are somehow inseparable, and yet public discussion of the matter is often inane. Even various Christians who have spoken about the "born-again" phenomenon, have failed to grasp the issues involved.

The Islamic revival also sheds new light on the relationship between faith and politics. The fall of the Shah and the rise of a theocratic Islamic Republic in Iran, the internal Islamic resistance to the Soviet invasion of Afghanistan, and turmoil throughout the Middle East are major manifestations of an Islamic "third way" between Eastern communism and Western technological progressivism. The rise of this "third way" has great implications for the future of international life.

Another example of renewed interest in religion and politics came by way of Radio Moscow on July 22, 1979. The "Moscow Mailbag" show presented a foreign listener's question: "Why isn't the USSR religious?" The Soviet commentator replied that accepting religion implies accepting the existence of a supernatural being, a being which would control mankind. At the mercy of such Providence, all men would resign themselves to accept whatever happened. The vast majority of Soviet citizens are atheists, the Moscow commentator asserted, because they believe that man takes events into his own hands in order to control his own destiny. This Radio Moscow commentary is a garbled indication that the Soviet ideologue knows that his greatest enemy is the sovereign God of Scripture.

Today millions of people in various parts of the world are concerned with the relationship of religious values to public affairs. Yet deeper insight into the meaning of this vital relationship is often missing. Thus, attempts to influence politics with religion are often ambiguous.

Historical study might bring some clarity and insight to this matter. In the hope of doing so, these pages have been written. Abraham Kuyper (1837-1920) is best known in the English-speaking world as a theologian and devotionalist, but in the present study he emerges as a Christian statesman. His roles as theologian and statesman were not contradictory, but were typical of his life-long attempt to relate the Christian faith to modern secular culture. Kuyper was a born-again child of God eager to glorify the Lord in his public and private concerns. With his many accomplishments in various fields, "Abraham the Mighty" was one of the great modern leaders in the Evangelical and Reformed traditions of Christianity. Yet his life and significant accomplishments are largely unknown outside of his own country. This small study is an attempt to present important aspects of his public career which are related to his Christian view of reality.

This great and powerful personality had a profound influence over like-minded Christians in the Netherlands from 1870 to 1960, and to a lesser extent, even up to the present. The keys to his success were his unusual talents as preacher, public speaker, journalist, creative thinker, organizer, and administrator. Reformed common people formed his political (and ecclesiastical) constituency in a time of deep spiritual reawakening. This spiritual revitalization was rooted in the Evangelical Awakening which began in Western Europe in the early nineteenth century, after the rise to dominance of secular unbelief generated by the French Revolution and the Napoleonic conquest of Europe. Kuyper preached the total claims of the Gospel. He enthusiastically proclaimed that obedience to the Christ of the Scriptures brought about personal salvation and social renewal. Above all, this great leader was a powerful evangelist for the Kingdom of God and a militant defender of the faith.

Kuyper's simple yet profound Christian vision was based upon a deep faith in Christ as the King over the entire cosmos. The exercise of this Christian vision in public affairs can be called "political spirituality" — the ability to discern the directions sin and grace take in public affairs. Political spirituality is an integrated Christian attitude which enriches both thought and action. This book will present and briefly evaluate aspects of Kuyper's public career as examples of political spirituality. This attitude of political spirituality must not be confused with Kuyper's political tactics. Tactics change as times and situations differ, "political spirituality" remains part of a Christian's obligation to do all things to the glory of God. The attitude of Christians towards secularized society determines what they think and do.

The pages that follow emphasize the historical context, based on documentary evidence, of what happened many years ago in a small country on the North Sea. From this Dutch context, and from one leader's experience, the Kuyperian perspective emerged. This book is not a biography; rather, it describes important episodes which demonstrate concretely Kuyper's political spirituality. The book is divided according to the three major divisions in Kuyper's public career: party leader, prime minister, and elder statesman. Examining his experiences during these three periods enables the historian to chart the genesis of his ideas, to see how he tried to put them into practice while in power, and then to note the battle scars and mature reflection of his later years.

Throughout his career Kuyper used Christian media (in his day, the daily newspaper, other publications, and the speaker's platform), Christian education on all levels, and Christian organizations (such as political parties, labor unions, publishing companies, and educational institutions) to achieve a visible Christian presence in a pluralistic society. His own political stance opposed all forms of humanism (such as Conservatism, Liberalism, Centrism, and Marxism). Kuyper was a Protestant Christian Democrat who tried to create a "third way" between individualism and collectivism. In this sense the Kuyperian political option has many formal similarities with the contemporary Christian Democratic movement in Europe associated with the work of the Frenchman Robert Schuman (1886-1963), the German Konrad Adenauer (1876-1967), the Italian Alcide de Gasperi (1881-1954), and the continuing influence of the continent-wide Christian Democratic federation known as the European People's Party.

Although this book emphasizes the strength of Kuyper's political spirituality, at times I will also note some of his weaknesses. Since Kuyper himself touched so many disciplines, this book may be of value not only to historians and theologians, but also to philosophers, political scientists, sociologists, and others concerned with the question of the application of Christian values in a secular world. Kuyper's career cannot be a blueprint for current attempts at Christian politics; however, his political spirituality in its historical context is a modest but very important contribution to the current discussion on "born-again" politics. Sanctified attitudes are essential to proper Christian action.

To learn about Kuyper and his surroundings, I carried out extensive research on his newspaper journalism at the Protestant Documentation Center associated with the Free University of Amsterdam, and I visited his home and the Second Chamber of the States-General (parliament), both in The Hague.

I want to express my thanks to the following gentlemen who were kind enough to answer my questions about the Kuyper tradition: George Puchinger, Hendrik Algra, Willem Aantjes, Hans de Boer, Herman Dooyeweerd, A. Th. van Deursen, Herman Ridderbos, and Cornelius Van Til.

The photographs used in this book are courtesy of George Puchinger, director of the Free University's Protestant Documentation Center, and the late Hans Rookmaaker.

The body of this book first appeared as a series of sixteen articles published between June 1979 and March 1981 in *Renewal*, a Reformed fortnightly periodical now published as *Christian Renewal*. The whole project was undertaken as part of my work in the Abraham Kuyper Chair of Dordt College's Studies Institute. My special thanks go to Bernard J. Haan, to the editors of *Renewal* and to John B. Hulst, the Institute's director. Appreciation must also be expressed to George Puchinger, Jan de Bruyn, H. Evan Runner, James A. De Jong, and Richard Lovelace for reading the manuscript and offering helpful comments. My thanks to Pat Weaver for her excellent editorial assistance. I am grateful for encouragement and for three big volumes of Kuyper's parliamentary speeches received from the late Abraham Warnaar Jzn., formerly a member of the Central Committee of the Anti-Revolutionary Party.* Final responsibility for the strengths and weaknesses of this book is mine alone.

McKendree R. Langley

*I would like to thank my wife Sandra for her love and encouragement throughout the various stages of this project. My daughter Tacye and my son Kenny helped me keep my sense of humor as we looked at Kuyper photographs together.

Kuyper as Party Leader

1879-1901

hg12

Abraham Kuyper as editor of *The Standard* daily newspaper in 1872 (Documentatiecentrum, Vrije Universiteit te Amsterdam courtesy of its director, Dr. George Puchinger).

Chapter 1

Anti-Revolutionary Centennial

"*E*VEN IN THE REALM OF POLITICS, the Anti-Revolutionary movement confesses the eternal principles of God's Word; state authority is bound to the ordinances of God only in the conscience of public officials and not directly so bound nor through the pronouncements of any Church." With this firm commitment to biblical normativity the Anti-Revolutionary Party was formally organized as the first national political party in the Netherlands. The date was April 3, 1879—more than a century ago—and the place was a congress center in Utrecht.

Dr. Abraham Kuyper opened the party congress with a few remarks about the significant contribution of G. Groen van Prinsterer (1801-1876) to Anti-Revolutionary theory and practice since 1840. He mentioned a necessary break with the humanist Conservatives in 1871 and the death of Groen in 1876. Because of these factors, Kuyper said, and because of the continued growth of secular political groups, Christians needed a more definite party organization to maintain and expand their voice in public life. After justifying the establishment several years earlier of a provisional Anti-Revolutionary Central Committee, Kuyper answered

9

various questions about the party's past, present, and future.

The Anti-Revolutionary Program of twenty-one principles was then unanimously adopted by the Congress. Quoted above is the third principle, which affirms the normativity of the ordinances of God found in Scripture and also in creation. Other principles affirmed God as the ultimate source of sovereign authority over the state, updated the Reformation faith for today, called for the complete separation of church and state, and made a firm commitment to Christian social reforms in a democratic parliamentary context. A clear call that the Gospel have unhindered influence in national life, the Program appealed to Christian conscience. The articulation of these principles is reminiscent of Calvin's exposition of the Moral Law of God in Book II of the *Institutes of the Christian Religion* (1559).

After a full discussion, the party constitution was ratified. Article One stated:

> A Central Committee of Anti-Revolutionary Voter's Clubs exists with headquarters in Utrecht. The goal of the Central Committee is to promote national unity among Anti-Revolutionaries by union and cooperation. It also seeks to disseminate the Anti-Revolutionary principles among the voters by encouraging the use of private initiative in the electoral districts.

Thus the party loosely united local voters' clubs which subscribed to the Anti-Revolutionary Program of Principles and agreed to follow the advice of the Central Committee during election campaigns. Hardly monolithic, the party functioned as a federation of like-minded local political organizations.

A fourteen-member permanent Central Committee was then elected, including Dr. Kuyper as chairman and Prof. B.J.L. Baron de Geer van Jutfaas and Jonkheer Alexander F. de Savornin Lohman as legal advisors. These three top officials comprised the Advisory Commission—the party's political leadership. During the next one hundred years, the party deeply influenced the nation both in "political spirituality" (the ability to see both sin and grace in public affairs) and in Christian action.

The deeper significance of the Anti-Revolutionary centennial lies in the past and in the future. In 1847 Groen van Prinsterer's penetrating major work, *Unbelief and Revolution*, analyzed and gave a Christian alternative to the secularization of culture. Humanistic unbelief, in its various revolutionary, progressive, *status quo*, and reactionary forms, dominated Europe. His slogan "The Gospel versus the Revolution," asserted the antithesis between all forms of secular humanist politics and the Reformed faith. Groen always sought to defend the faith from this onslaught of secularistic unbelief with a political spirituality: "The preaching of the Gospel is practical even when it causes opposition. The articulation of Anti-Revolutionary truths is practical even when the Revolution principle is dominant . . . This continual witness is itself dynamic action. The preaching of justice in the face of continual injustice is not superfluous."

Both Groen and Kuyper sought to defend the time-and-space, historical fact of the Christ of the Scriptures against those who would separate the "Jesus of history" from the "Christ of faith." In an autobiographical fragment of 1873, *In Confidence*, Kuyper wrote that his life's goal was to defend the Christian faith from the attacks of unbelief in both church and state. He was determined to present a total Christian alternative on a Reformed basis. Defense, witness, and alternative were for Kuyper inseparable.

Between 1840 and 1888 secular Liberals dominated Dutch politics and their unbelieving modernist colleagues were tolerated in the Dutch Reformed Church. Groen and Kuyper stepped upon this scene; their witness resulted in a burgeoning of Reformed faith in all areas of life. Kuyper gave a rallying cry in his daily newspaper, *The Standard*, on June 7, 1873:

God has spoken.
There is a revelation of His will which we have in God's Word. On this basis we demand that the pronouncement of God's Word be obeyed in each clash of principles. Human inference or discretion is only to be decisive where God's Word is unclear.

Everyone agrees that human insight must yield to God's pronouncements. The disagreement begins because our opponents do not believe God Himself has spoken while we confess that He has spoken. The Gospel versus the Revolution! This is the conviction that we must be able to declare in order to awaken the proper type of belief. We only ask for this right, but this is what we are denied.

The secularization of public life which Groen and Kuyper saw flowing out of the Enlightenment and the French Revolution has spread from Europe to the entire Western world and beyond. Those throughout the world who are concerned to defend and proclaim the Christ of the Scripture and His rule can profit from the Anti-Revolutionary legacy. This pattern of integrating faith and culture, this example of political stewardship which attests to the abiding relevance of biblical normativity, gives us courage and perspective as we face an uncertain future. Kuyper was obedient in the situation of 1879. Will we be faithful in our situation today?

Kuyper as a young Member of Parliament in 1875 (Documentatiecentrum, Vrije Universiteit te Amsterdam courtesy of its director, Dr. George Puchinger).

Chapter 2

The Events of 1879

"**O**UR SYMPATHY IS WITH the Anti-Revolutionaries because at present, among Protestants, it is only the orthodox segment that is being harmed by the neglect of the great principles of both equality before the law and freedom of education." So declared forty-two-year-old Dr. Abraham Kuyper in *The Standard* daily newspaper on June 20, 1879. He was explaining the larger reason for the national formation of the Anti-Revolutionary Party the previous April. The party was not founded nor the principles adopted simply because they were intellectually satisfying. Both were deemed necessary to provide a Reformed political alternative to the dominance of an unbelieving Liberal bourgeoisie.

During the 1870s the Liberal Party was split between *status quo* and reformist wings. The Conservative Party, almost indistinguishable from *status quo* Liberalism, was suffering a lingering political demise. But both Liberals and Conservatives were united in their quest for the supremacy of secular politics and by their unyielding opposition to an integrated political spirituality. Set basically on a secular two-party system, they were hostile to the legitimate attempts of Calvinists and Catholics to organize politically. A multi-party system which would contain both secular and confessional parties brought strong opposition from secular politicians because it threatened their power. Liberals, for example, claimed that the introduction of Christian parties into public life would revive sectarian hatreds and return the Netherlands to the Inquisition. Yet when the Anti-Revolutionary Party and other confessional parties were established, more true liberty for all resulted, a far cry from inquisition.

Election

1879 was an election year. In the statement of June 20 (given above), Kuyper claimed that the Liberal government of Prime Minister J. Kappeyne van de Coppello had failed to do justice to the hundreds of thousands of Anti-Revolutionaries in two areas:

1. equality before the law (widening the vote);
2. freedom of education (Christian parents' just request to be relieved of the requirement to pay for both the public school and the Christian school).

During May and early June the Anti-Revolutionary Central Committee, under Kuyper's leadership, brought discipline to the network of the party's voters' clubs. The Program of Principles adopted at Utrecht on April 3 clearly identified the party position in the campaign. The Anti-Revolutionary principles dramatized the Christian conviction that normativity for politics, as for all of life, came from the Bible. Therefore Christians had to reject the relativistic values of popular sovereignty as articulated by the secular Liberals and Conservatives.

As the leading Anti-Revolutionary daily, *The Standard* stated on May 1, May 12, and June 9 that its three major campaign issues were:

1. the party's independence from other political groups and the government;
2. the need to widen the vote to give more adequate

parliamentary representation to the common people; and

3. opposition to Prime Minister Kappeyne van de Coppello's Primary Education Law of August 27, 1878, which reaffirmed the requirement that Christian parents pay double to send their children to Christian schools.

The Central Committee then issued a long list of approved Anti-Revolutionary parliamentary candidates. The local voters' clubs were busy with the grass-roots campaigning. It was a coordinated national effort.

Election day was June 10 and the run-off elections were held on June 24. The Anti-Revolutionaries elected nine candidates to the powerful Second Chamber of the States-General (parliament) in The Hague. The Catholics elected nine, the Conservatives three, and the Liberals twenty-two. Since national elections were held every two years, only one-half of the seats were open. After these elections of 1879, then, the composition of the Second Chamber was as follows: Anti-Revolutionaries 12, Catholics 17, Conservatives 6, and Liberals 51. Among the Anti-Revolutionaries elected were Jonkheer P.J. Elout van Soeterwoude, who shortly thereafter became chairman of his party's parliamentary delegation, L.W.C. Keuchenius, who became Minister of Colonies in the first Calvinist-Catholic cabinet in 1888, and Jonkheer Alexander F. de Savornin Lohman, who later broke with Kuyper in 1894 to eventually form another party called the Christian Historical Union.

Cabinet Crisis

During this summer of 1879 a governmental crisis arose in the Kappeyne Cabinet due to disagreements between *status quo* and progressive cabinet ministers. The Liberal Party controlled 51 seats in the Second Chamber, and the other parties controlled 35. Though the Liberals had a paper majority of 16, the split between the Liberal

factions finally caused the Kappeyne Cabinet to resign.
On August 21 the new government was announced, an
extraparliamentary cabinet headed by Baron C. Th. van
Lynden van Sandenburg and included Liberals and Conservatives. Van Lynden van Sandenburg had once been
an Anti-Revolutionary, but service in the two previous
Conservative Heemskerk Cabinets had caused him to
alter his views. On August 22, *The Standard* editorialist,
with a note of sadness, gave up all hope that Prime
Minister Van Lynden van Sandenburg would support full
financial pluralism for primary education.

A week later, on August 28, the Anti-Revolutionary
Central Committee met at Dr. Kuyper's house to consider
the party's stance toward the new government. After
discussion, the committee passed an unanimous resolution declaring opposition to the Van Lynden van Sandenburg Cabinet because of its composition and viewpoint.
The committee also decided that the party would continue to act on the basis of its Program of Principles.

Conclusions

How did Kuyper then view the formation of the Anti-
Revolutionary Party in the light of these political events?
By August 13, the party was too influential to be ignored.
Kuyper pointed out the following five accomplishments:

1. The formal adoption of the Program of Principles,
   which in his estimation was the most important
   characteristic of the party. Both friend and foe
   could see what Anti-Revolutionary citizens stood
   for.
2. The unity of various Anti-Revolutionary newspapers, which would contribute to a unified perspective on public affairs.
3. The organization of the Anti-Revolutionary
   voters' clubs under the Central Committee, gua-
   ranteeing party unity and political effectiveness.
4. The steady growth of support among the voters.

5. The vindication of the tactic of party independence from all forms of political humanism by seeking grass-roots support rather than compromising principle to gain entrance to Liberal or Conservative governments.

Three conclusions can be drawn from the events of 1879:

1. Kuyper saw the articulation of Reformed political principles as the most important contribution made by Christian politics. Political spirituality—the Christian attitude behind the evaluation of public events—had to be articulated in clear and accessible terms.

2. The national organization of the party under the Central Committee was Kuyper's tactic for working out his political spirituality. While tactics vary in different situations, the Christian is always obliged to work out, in a practical way, his integrated political spirituality.

3. Kuyper recognized that both the attitude of Reformed political spirituality and a viable tactic were necessary to articulate and defend the rights of Christian citizens from the debilitating policies of a hostile, secular political establishment. The Christian faith was under vigorous attack by men who felt biblical normativity had little or nothing to do with the way the nation was governed. Kuyper engaged himself in Christian politics because obedience to the Lordship of Christ and the future of the nation were at stake.

Groen van Prinsterer: "The Gospel versus the Revolution" (courtesy of the late
Prof. Hans Rookmaaker and the Rijksprentenkabinet, Amsterdam).

Chapter 3

Anti-Revolutionary Principles

"**P**EOPLE DON'T READ ENOUGH. They don't make the effort to reflect on a question seriously. They are sometimes called Anti-Revolutionary without really understanding what the Anti-Revolutionary principles are." On September 1, 1879, this complaint was published in *The Standard*, a daily newspaper under the editorship of Dr. Abraham Kuyper. Above all, Kuyper wanted friend and foe to understand the position of the Anti-Revolutionary Party. The method he chose was to publicize the Program of Principles adopted the previous April. In every political contest Kuyper sought to clarify the antithesis between the basic principles of Christianity and the basic principles of humanism. His journalistic efforts in *The Standard* between 1872 and 1919 always emphasized the clash of principles (as he himself remarked as early as June 7, 1873). Clearly articulated principles and their implications which were worked out in a brilliant journalistic enterprise undergirded the development of the Kuyperian world-view and mass party. Certainly Kuyper's important work as party organizer and chairman cannot be overlooked. But it was his careful relation of the complexities of public life to the Anti-Revolutionary principles which was the key to the party's lasting significance. Principles gave structure to a viable political spirituality; principial discussion is an important part of the Anti-Revolutionary legacy.

"If attention is given to principles," Kuyper wrote on April 23, 1875, "then you will have the ear of the nation. But if you as a politician are concerned only with the details of legislation, then only about ten journalists and a few other public officials will pay attention to what you say." Kuyper tried to focus political debate on the clash of basic principles. *Principle* would distinguish truth from half-truth and falsehood. The clash of principles would bring attention to Christian principles. Kuyper believed that writing about the clash of opposing principles would be a way of educating the people about public affairs and of integrating Reformed Christianity with culture on a normative basis.

Groen's Contribution

But the real father of Anti-Revolutionary principles was G. Groen van Prinsterer — historian, statesman, Gospel-confessor. Principles seem to leap out of the pages of his major work, *Unbelief and Revolution* (1847). Groen sought to distinguish the truth of God from the attacks of an age of unbelief, and he drew comfort from the cloud of witnesses from Bible times to the modern age. Above all, he emphasized, we must struggle to articulate an independent Christian viewpoint in our own times. This independent viewpoint must be based upon our unconditional subjection to the Holy Scriptures. God's Word is the basis for law, ethics, authority, and freedom for individuals as well as for governments. Viewing history through biblical glasses, Groen saw the great importance of the Reformation. By contrast, secular humanists who saw history through the glasses of would-be autonomous man concluded that the French Revolution was the great historical watershed. Groen called such humanist thought anti-biblical and anti-historical.

Groen dealt with the matter of normativity primarily in the first three lectures and in the conclusion of *Unbelief and Revolution*. After a long discussion on the relationship of the Bible to human history, he made it clear that he was basing his Anti-Revolutionary world-view on the complete normativity of the Bible. The Christian has the Holy Scriptures as his guide. "The Bible is the infallible standard" (p. 29). The wisdom of the finest pagan classicists of antiquity is a mirage when compared to the Gospel. The fear of the Lord is the beginning of wisdom. The doctrine of salvation through faith in the divine-historic Jesus Christ includes the imputation of His righteousness, the new birth, and the Christian life of sanctification. Sin has permeated the unfolding of human culture so that history cannot be normative in the ultimate sense.

It is clear that Groen was not a conservative. The Jewish theocratic laws of the Old Testament have expired, and the Ten Commandments have continuing validity as seen in the light of the Gospel of Christ. No theocrat, Groen followed the pattern of John Calvin's analysis of the relationship of Old Testament law to New Testament Gospel (see Book II of the *Institutes of the Christian Religion*). Scripture sheds normative light on history, not vice versa. Principles are those truths deduced from Scripture which can be applied to given historical problems. In the process of the formulation of principles, Christian conscience must reflect on the relationship of special grace to common grace and on sin and historical distortion. Only then can justice be done to both Scripture and historical context. Groen's hermeneutical approach was rooted firmly in the Reformed tradition even though he was not always as systematic on these matters as we might like.

More light on the nature of Anti-Revolutionary principles is found in the correspondence Groen carried on with several influential people. On April 24, 1871, his old friend and Anti-Revolutionary parliamentarian, Jonkheer P.J. Elout van Soeterwoude, wrote that Groen's efforts were ecclesiastical, theological, and political, in other words, all-inclusive. "God has used your struggle," Elout continued, "to bring attention to the highest in-

terests of the nation but without the means to apply your
ideals." Bringing attention to the highest national interests was a clear reference to Groen's defense of Christian principles in public debate. It was true that Groen
was unable to translate the principles into the political
practice of government, but he had articulated those
principles, and Elout was very thankful for that contribution.

A second comment on Groen's principles came from
another friend, Baron B.J.L. de Geer van Jutphaas, law
professor at Utrecht University, on April 7, 1872. He
pointed out that those who were concerned about the
truth thankfully recognized Groen's profound contribution to politics, government, church, and school matters.
On every question or event, De Geer continued, his friend
brought light by his continual discussion and tireless
reflection. De Geer contrasted the Anti-Revolutionary
viewpoint with Liberalism, totalitarian Socialism and
theocratic political Catholicism. De Geer wished that
more people would hear Groen's Anti-Revolutionary
message. Three years later, on June 15, 1875, Prof. De
Geer wrote about the relationship of principles to educa-

Groen's home in The Hague (center) where he delivered the lectures in 1845-46
that were then published as *Unbelief and Revolution* (M.R. Langley).

tion. Public education, based upon the conviction that man is perfectible, was related to anti-Christian humanism in general and to modernist theology in particular. Christian education is based upon belief in human depravity and the need for conversion as the basis of true learning. De Geer outlined the conflict between these two pedagogical viewpoints.

Another clarification of the nature of Christian principles was given by Groen himself on June 16, 1875. Groen was advising Jonkheer J.L. de Jonge, an Anti-Revolutionary candidate for Parliament who had just won a seat from Middleburg but was not sure whether he should accept the mandate. Groen emphasized that Parliament was where the pulse of national life could be felt. In such a place, a Christian did not have to be an expert on every aspect of statecraft, but he did have an obligation to give a Christian witness concerning the highest interests of all the people in the issues debated. Moreover, given the fragmentation of the parties, even one vote could be decisive on the outcome of a motion.

The comments of Elout, De Geer, and Groen make it clear that Christian principles are (1) the result of reflection on Christianity and culture; (2) the product of the clash of Calvinism with humanism in the conscience of the Christian; (3) related to the realization that a view of man (either as perfectible or as in need of the Savior) is basic to all political perspectives; and (4) the outcome of the obligation to witness to the highest interests of peoples and nations.

Groen's concern for principles drove him to investigate the relation of biblical normativity to the common grace structures of creation and history and especially to the exercise of political sovereignty. In other words, the statesman from The Hague was concerned to articulate a properly normed, Protestant and democratic credo which was applicable to public affairs in the modern world.

Kuyper's Contribution

So important was the articulation of the Anti-Revolutionary principles that Abraham Kuyper spent most of the decade of the 1870s working on the project. As stated in the theological journal, *The Herald*, on January 1, 1871, Kuyper sought to create an independent Christian option in politics, a third way, distinct from Conservatism and Liberalism. Even in 1871 this Calvinist leader was looking ahead fifty years (to 1921!) and working for the wider influence of the Reformed principles. Kuyper saw beyond daily events to the long-term effects of reformation. Such long-range vision is needed today. In fact, the lack of it may be one reason that Christian impact on contemporary culture is so marginal.

In the first editorial in *The Standard* on April 1, 1872, Kuyper eloquently declared that the standard of God's Word was to be raised in national affairs. He followed Calvin in declaring that the Bible acts as eyeglasses which enable man to "see" who God is and how to understand a creation which has fallen into sin (October 29, 1873). The Christian statesman, Kuyper maintained, formulated principles that bring revealed normativity to bear on the problems of his age. Ultimately this process is a matter of Christian conscience, but it reflects both biblical truth and current political reality (November 7, 1873).

The Anti-Revolutionary Program of April 3, 1879, contained twenty-one principles. The first five principles were foundational and the remainder articulated reforms considered basic to the party's cause at that time. Our attention is on the first five principles.

"The Anti-Revolutionary, Christian Historical movement represents the essence of national Netherlandic history: the Reformation tradition applied in relevant ways in our own day." The first principle is a clear appeal to the Reformed faith, political reform, nationalist consciousness, and resistance to tyranny. The notion of updating the Reformation is biblical and progressive, not reactionary.

"The source of sovereign authority is found in God alone and not in the will of the people nor in human law. Popular sovereignty is rejected while the sovereignty of the House of Orange is affirmed as under God's historical leading, culminating in the re-establishment of Dutch independence in 1813 and in the drafting of the national Constitution." This second principle declares that ultimate sovereignty belongs to God alone. Within this context, He delegates political sovereignty to legitimate leaders, in this case the House of Orange, in a constitutional framework. This principle is an application of Romans 13.

The third principle is perhaps the most basic one in the entire Anti-Revolutionary program: "Even in the realm of politics the Anti-Revolutionary movement confesses the eternal principles of God's Word; state authority is bound to the ordinances of God only in the conscience of public officials and not directly so bound, nor through the pronouncements of any church." This statement professes that the Bible is the normative standard for politics; Biblical truth must be articulated in principles relevant to a given situation. The ordinances of God (the law structures) are revealed in principle in Scripture and in detail in the creation, but are applied only by means of Christian conscience. Kuyper thus avoided theocratic oppression on the one hand and antinomian licentiousness on the other. Only through an organized political movement which appealed to Christian conscience would Kuyper attempt to apply the commands of God to public life. His conviction concerning the depravity of man—including Christian leaders— caused Kuyper to work within a democratic, constitutional framework. And the task of the state to promulgate public justice was always to be distinguished from the spiritual authority of the church.

The fourth principle concerns public impartiality

towards organized religion: "In a Christian (non-religionless) state, the government, as the servant of God, is to glorify God's name by (1) removing all administrative and legislative hindrances to the full expression of the Gospel in national life; (2) refraining from any direct interference with the spiritual development of the nation, for that is beyond government's competence; (3) treating equally all churches, religious organizations, and citizens regardless of their views on eternal matters; and (4) recognizing in the conscience a limit to state power in so far as conscience is presumed to be honorable." This principle is based on the presupposition that life is inescapably religious in character and that democratic social pluralism is essential to the creation of governments' impartiality. The separation of church and state is fundamental to the unique and separate tasks of both institutions.

The fifth principle deals with Sunday legislation and judicial oaths: "The Anti-Revolutionary movement confesses that the government rules by the grace of God from whom its governing authority is derived. The state has the right, therefore, to require the use of the oath (in court) and to keep the Lord's Day free. It is also in the national interest to revise the existing Sunday legislation to allow for rest on this day from all state functions . . ." This statement seeks to maintain Sunday as the civic day of rest in a society with a strong Christian tradition.

Conclusion

Groen and Kuyper, spokesmen of political spirituality, articulated Reformed principles, and thereby avoided the dead ends of both theocratic coercion and clericalism in politics. They followed the tradition of John Calvin, who defended the validity of the Ten Commandments when seen in the light of the Gospel and reflected in a principled life of obedience to Christ. Only the Bible illumines the meaning of creation and history. As both men saw, God's truth must be brought to bear on the secular culture of the modern age.

Those concerned with public affairs today would do well to reflect on this Anti-Revolutionary legacy in order to articulate a contemporary statement of Christian principles which would give direction to our post-Christian age.

The Kuyper family in the 1890s (Documentatiecentrum, Vrije Universiteit te Amsterdam courtesy of its director, Dr. George Puchinger).

Chapter 4

Defense
and Encouragement

THE 1880s WERE A STORMY PERIOD for both the Netherlands and the Anti-Revolutionary Party. Many changes took place which created a new situation. In the midst of the many new tensions Dr. Abraham Kuyper, as chairman of the Anti-Revolutionary Party, had to defend his leadership from internal attack and encourage the party faithful. His perseverance paved the way, in 1888, for the formation of the first Anti-Revolutionary-Catholic government, the Mackay Cabinet.

A brief review of some of the most important new developments of the 1880s will clarify Kuyper's response to the tensions he faced.

Background

On October 20, 1880 Kuyper opened the Free University of Amsterdam with a magnificent address on "Sphere Sovereignty." The central theme of this speech was the cosmic rule of Christ over the various aspects of the creation. Christ delegates responsibility to diverse spheres which are not to be taken over by the modern centralizing state. Limited sovereignty is given to such "spheres" as family, church, state, education, private associations, business, trade, society, nature, and the individual person. Kuyper stressed that the legitimate task of the state is

to coordinate, with justice, the proper functioning of all
the spheres. The state must not repress the freedoms
within these spheres, but rather, must insure the proper
functioning of internal liberty. In this Free University in-
augural, Kuyper then affirmed that the sphere of education is independent from governmental control. This
theory of "sphere sovereignty" provided a clear rationale
for the establishment of private Christian organizations
such as the Free University, *The Standard* daily
newspaper, Christian ecclesiastical denominations and
the Anti-Revolutionary Party, each of which had its own
task in its own sphere. This theory allowed Christians to
work in all areas of created reality for God's glory. Both in
theory and in practice young people could be educated to
take part in the growing Reformed cause in church, state,
and other areas of endeavor.

In the same year, 1880, Mgr. Herman Schaepman
was elected to Parliament as a Catholic representative
from Breda. Mgr. Schaepman was the first Catholic
clergyman admitted to the Second Chamber. Three years
later Schaepman published his Catholic political program
which helped to give ideological form to the Catholic party. It was Kuyper's gradually growing friendship with
Mgr. Schaepman that formed the basis of the Anti-
Revolutionary-Catholic political coalition which
dominated Dutch public life for more than a generation.
Both parties wanted to see realized a truly pluralistic
educational system instead of the intolerant monolithic
system favored by the secular parties. This coalition
would eventually make it possible for Kuyper himself to
serve as prime minister of the Netherlands from
1901-1905.

The first Social Democratic political congress was
held in 1882 under the leadership of an ex-Lutheran
pastor-turned-atheist, F. Domela Nieuwenhuis. Socialist
political clubs had been set up in Amsterdam, The
Hague, Haarlem, and Rotterdam, where there were large
numbers of poor urban workers. Nieuwenhuis himself

edited the Socialist paper *Equal Rights* in downtown Amsterdam just a few blocks from the office of *The Standard*, edited by Abraham Kuyper. The entry of Nieuwenhuis into Parliament from the Frisian district of Schoterland in 1888 marked the beginning of Socialist representation in that body. Socialist demonstrations and strikes were held with increasing frequency.

From 1883 to 1888 the last Conservative government held power with the extra-parliamentary Heemskerk Cabinet. In the parliamentary elections of 1884, 23 Anti-Revolutionaries, 18 Catholics, 3 Conservatives, and 42 Liberals were elected. For the first time in many years, the Liberals were in a minority, since the non-Liberal parties held 44 seats. Heemskerk stayed in power, but the time was drawing closer for a cabinet of the confessional parties. Shortly thereafter the Liberals temporarily regained a majority of 47 to 39.

By an act of Parliament in 1884, Queen Emma, the mother of Princess Wilhelmina, age 4, was declared to be the future Regent of the Netherlands because King Willem III was very old and there were no male heirs. This insured an orderly transferal of Dutch sovereignty.

In spite of the recent Liberal decline, in early 1885 a Jewish lawyer, J.A. Levy, founded the Liberal Union Party as the national organization of a federation of local Liberal voters' clubs. The Liberals did not want to be left unorganized since the Anti-Revolutionaries, Catholics, and even the Socialists were busy bringing discipline to their parties.

During 1886 and 1887 the 'Doleantie" took place in which Kuyper and other church leaders led a great body of orthodox believers out of the modernistic Dutch Reformed Church. This body eventually became the confessional Reformed Churches of the Netherlands. Significant political repercussions followed this great ecclesiastical event.

A final major political change: in 1887 various legislative adjustments and constitutional reforms were passed into law providing for the parliamentary Second Chamber representation to be increased from 86 to 100 and the First Chamber (Senate) representation from 39 to 50.

Defense in 1885

A special Anti-Revolutionary party congress was held in The Hague on July 2, 1885. Many delegates had attended the meeting of the Free University held in the same auditorium on the previous day. A party congress was the party's parliament in which representatives of the various local voters' clubs, affiliated newspapers, and Anti-Revolutionary office-holders were represented. The congress was to discuss proposed constitutional changes in relation to education and state funding for churches. But by the day it began, the real issue at hand was criticism of Kuyper's leadership both by a former central committee member, Rev. S.H. Buitendijk, and by the well-known editorialist, Dr. A.W. Bronsveld. These critics charged that Kuyper was leading the party in the wrong direction.

Kuyper used this important opportunity to defend his own leadership and to ask the congress to decide whether he should resign or stay on. His speech revealed some of his own deepest motivations. He emphasized the great impact of Groen van Prinsterer's Christian witness on his life. Against the advice of several short-sighted Evangelicals in 1868, Kuyper had kept admiring Groen as *the* Christian leader who pointed the nation away from the growing cancer of secularization. How moving it was for this young pastor to meet Groen and to become his friend. The elder statesman himself faced the hostility of those same individualistic Evangelicals.

Kuyper referred to the years of friendship, conversation, and correspondence with Groen as a great honor, for they enabled him to become thoroughly acquainted with the Anti-Revolutionary world-view. (The Groen-Kuyper correspondence, 1864-1876, published in 1937, confirms this statement.) Kuyper's apprenticeship with Groen helped him prepare for the future. Groen stressed the continuing importance of both Christian education and a confessional church. He approved his young associate's draft of a Christian political program when the latter entered Parliament in 1874 and, during the last year of his life (1875-76), encouraged the preparations for the founding of the Free University.

Kuyper then suddenly declared that while he had been recuperating from overwork in May 1876 in the Swiss Alps, he had dreamed that Groen had been carried by angels to heaven. Later he received the sad news that Groen had indeed gone to be with the Lord. By the time Kuyper returned to the Netherlands in May, 1877, he was convicted afresh of the veracity of the Reformed faith and of the urgency of bringing more party organization to the Anti-Revolutionary movement. The party needed a program and a viable central committee to provide effective national leadership.

Surprisingly, Kuyper then confessed that upon re-reading his *Standard* journalism for the preceding years, he had seen that much of what he had written had not reflected enough of the Lord's Spirit. He hoped to improve. He wanted the proposed Free University to provide the necessary Christian scholarship for the future of both the party and the government. He ended by noting that the Program of Anti-Revolutionary Principles was the basis for discussion even when disputes arose within the party. He urged party unity on the basis of mutual Christian love. Then he retired from the podium.

Elections for chairman and legal advisor of the Central Committee were then held. The results for chairman were 112 votes for Kuyper and one vote for L.W.C. Keuchenius, and for legal advisor there were 109 votes for Jonkheer Alexander F. de Savornin Lohman and one vote for Keuchenius. A motion urging Kuyper to accept the chairmanship for the good of the party brought enthusiastic approval from the audience. Kuyper then thanked the delegates for their confidence in him and vowed to continue to serve the Lord as party chairman.

Encouragement

The tradition that the chairman should bring a message of encouragement to party congresses began in the 1880s. This was in keeping with the chairman's task of developing long-range vision and policy.

One of the first inspirational messages of this type was delivered by Kuyper on August 18, 1887 to a party congress held at Utrecht. There are three stages of the Christian life, Kuyper began. The first period begins with the conversion of a heart to Christ. In this period of immaturity the child of God is still entangled in worldliness. In the second period he turns away from worldly cares in order to meditate more fully on his Lord and Savior. Many Christians going through this stage fall into a false mysticism, Kuyper emphasized. During the third stage, one of greater maturity and balance, the believer recognizes that even clothing, spices, and jobs—indeed, everything—is from the Lord and thus in everything His Name must be glorified. Each Christian has his own calling which obligates him to use his talents responsibly to glorify God.

Kuyper pointed out that the many evangelical believers who remain in the second stage feel that politics is to be avoided as corrupting and ungodly. Such Christians give over their legitimate responsibilities to the control of satan and to unconverted men. This hyperspiritual fear of politics leads to more sinfulness in the public arena. But the balanced Christian who proceeds to the third stage recognizes that not only the invididual soul, but also the nation belongs to the Lord! He thankfully seeks to serve the King of kings even in politics.

Kuyper mentioned the pioneering work of the Calvinist leaders Willem Bilderdijk, Isaac Da Costa, and Groen van Prinsterer which during the previous fifty years had marked the beginnings of a national spiritual renewal. Now it was bearing fruit in Christian initiatives in politics, education, the press, and literature. Kuyper thoughtfully remarked that it was not, in England, Scotland, or America, but in Holland that Christians were able to engage in meaningful Christian politics. The Lord had bestowed a special honor on this small country on the North Sea. This work of reformation depended as fully on God's grace as did Ezekiel's dry bones that came to life. The Anti-Revolutionary Party, Kuyper concluded, needed this unifying reliance on the grace of the Lord and the common vision of political spirituality.

A few months later the party made two historically important decisions. First, it decided on December 20, 1887 to cooperate with the Catholic Party in the coming political campaign on the issue of educational pluralism, while maintaining its own independent party stance and election platform. The motion on cooperation was drawn up by Jonkheer de Savornin Lohman. This decision made possible the Mackay Cabinet of 1888 and those of later Right coalition governments. The Anti-Revolutionary delegates also passed an important resolution on February 15, 1888 regretting the loss of members who resigned from the party over church issues resulting from the church separation known as the Doleantie. It was affirmed that their contribution to the struggles against unbelief, secularization, and discrimination would be missed. Kuyper had previously declared that he did not want the party to become an arena for church disputes among orthodox believers.

Afterthoughts

1. Kuyper's friendship with Groen was of crucial importance in his growth to Christian maturity. Any attempt to understand Kuyper and his position must include a careful evaluation of the influence of Groen. What Kuyper did was to popularize and enrich in new ways the Anti-Revolutionary world-view found in *Unbelief and Revolution* (1847). Groen developed this up-dated Calvinist position with its inspiring defense of the faith and its political spirituality. Kuyper then took

the liberating message to the Reformed commoners by his powerful journalism, creative perspective, and dynamic public speaking. The organization and leadership of the Anti-Revolutionary Party took place under Kuyper's direction, but the genius behind this Reformed mass movement in church and state was really the historian-statesman, Groen van Prinsterer. It is a pity that he remains virtually unknown in Reformed circles. His book, *Unbelief and Revolution*, is still of crucial importance as a Reformed historical analysis of the roots of secularization and as an outline of an alternative Calvinist view of the world. Much more research on this great man of God must be undertaken in the coming years.

2. Kuyper was able to provide mature Christian leadership even in times of political and ecclesiastical stress. His statements of defense and encouragement were a powerful witness to the Lordship of Christ over both the individual and society. He wisely warned of the dangers of a false, individualistic mysticism, while he held high the Gospel banner as the only hope for true personal conversion and national renewal.

3. Kuyper the man is clearly visible in these speeches: a hard worker who collapsed from nervous exhaustion, a believer whose shaken faith was turned into strong conviction, an editorialist who repented of his journalistic aggressiveness when it may not have reflected the Spirit of the Lord, a political leader who thankfully accepted the party's mandate to carry on as chairman, and a Christian speaker who encouraged believers. Kuyper was a great man despite his own faults and his many political and ecclesiastical opponents. But through it all he gave a powerful testimony of his love for the Lord Jesus Christ and of his desire to serve Him in all of life.

Chapter 5

Between the Cross and the Second Coming

" *F* OR A NUMBER OF UNFORGETTABLE YEARS I had a
friendship with Groen van Prinsterer both by means
of personal conversations and through correspondence,
but I must tell you frankly: Groen never dreamed of the
possibility that one day four of our men would sit in the
Cabinet to defend and to work for the principles that are
holy to us."

These remarkable words were spoken by Dr.
Abraham Kuyper on May 12, 1891, during an Anti-
Revolutionary Party congress. These words reveal that
twelve short years after the death of Groen in 1876, the
first Anti-Revolutionary-Catholic government, the
Mackay Cabinet, took power in April, 1888. This govern-
ment of Baron Aeneas Mackay continued in office until
August 1891.

As a result of the parliamentary elections of early
1888 the political representation was as follows: Anti-
Revolutionaries, 28 seats; Catholics, 26; Liberals, 44;
with one Conservative and one Socialist (Domela
Nieuwenhuis). The Christian parties thus controlled 54
seats, while the secular parties held the remaining 46 seats
in the powerful parliamentary Second Chamber.

During April of 1888, the new cabinet took office
with the following members: Baron Aeneas Mackay

(Anti-Revolutionary, Prime Minister and Minister of Internal Affairs), Jonkheer K.A. Godin de Beaufort (Anti-Revolutionary, Finances), L.W.C. Keuchenius (Anti-Revolutionary, Colonies), J.P. Havelaar (Anti-Revolutionary, Waterworks), Jonkheer G.L.M.H. Ruijs de Beerenbroek (Catholic, Justice), J.W. Bergansius (Catholic, War), Jonkheer C. Hartsen (Old Conservative, Foreign Affairs) and H. Dyserinck (Old Conservative, Navy). In early 1890 Keuchenius left the Cabinet and Prime Minister Mackay took the colonial portfolio. Jonkheer Alexander F. de Savornin Lohman then joined the Cabinet as Minister of Internal Affairs, the department just vacated by Mackay.

Changes were also taking place in the House of Orange. In November of 1890, King Willem III died. His widow, Queen Emma, became the Regent for their young daughter Princess Wilhelmina (1880-1962).

There were two major legislative accomplishments of this first confessional cabinet: the School Law of 1889 and the Labor Law of 1889. Prime Minister Mackay, Minister of Internal Affairs, was the moving force behind the former law. It provided that private schools would receive public funding in proportion to the number of teachers and pupils in the schools, up to thirty percent of the total costs. This law was a step toward the complete public funding of public and private schools on the basis of equality, which was incorporated into the Dutch Constitution in 1917. The School Law of 1889 was an important accomplishment for a cabinet with school reform as its top priority.

The Catholic Minister of Justice, Jonkheer L.L.M.H. Ruijs de Beerenbroek, was the father of the Labor Law of 1889. Put forward on the basis of factory inspections conducted during 1886, this law was a modest beginning for sound legislation to protect workers. It prevented youths and women from engaging in excessively long work periods. Workers had to be at least twelve years old; women and those under sixteen could work no more than eleven hours a day. Night work was forbidden. Three inspectors were appointed to oversee the enforcement of this law. It is to the credit of this Right coalition cabinet that it was responsible for the first labor law, however modest, in Dutch legislative history.

At the beginning and again at the end of the term of office of the Mackay Cabinet, Dr. Abraham Kuyper gave addresses at the congresses of the Anti-Revolutionary Party. "Not the Liberty Tree but the Cross" was delivered on May 3, 1889, and "Maranatha" was presented on May 12, 1891. The two titles suggest the scope of Christian activity: between the cross and the second coming. Kuyper tried to clarify the political meaning of salvation and eschatology in the context of the modern world.

Given at the centennial of the French Revolution of 1789, "Not the Liberty Tree but the Cross" was Kuyper's perceptive analysis of the secularizing impact of that revolution. He pointed out the paradox of revolutionary idealism. Liberty was promised, and oppression followed. Equality was preached, but class war broke out. Fraternity was offered, but coercion became a part of life under Robespierre and the two Napoleons. Further revolutions broke out in 1830 and 1848, spreading from Paris to other countries. Europe was at war at various times during this period. Such a paradox existed, Kuyper maintained, because these secularists denied the innate depravity of the human heart. Enlightenment theory and revolutionary practice emphasized that only social structures were "bad." Destroy these structures, the humanists thought, and oppression would cease. But the Revolution was betrayed again and again because, Kuyper pointed out, sin governed the hearts of the successful street fighters. The revolutionists refused to bow before the sovereign God of men and nations. "Neither God nor master!" was their battle cry. Fundamentally the paradox of the Revolution was due to its anti-Christian bias. Moral standards were reversed: Robespierre described the Reign of Terror as the "War of Liberty against Despotism." But the pervasive myth of the perfectability of man turned liberation into genocide. In truth, it is from the heart, not from reason, that the issues of life come, in obedience or disobedience to the Lord of all. Kuyper saw that sin is fundamental to the rise of tyranny in history.

The chairman's second point: revolutionary idealism forms the basis of secular politics. The fundamental notion that autonomous man applies reason to culture to create humanist politics was in Kuyper's view, basic to Conservatism, Liberalism, Radicalism, Socialism, and Communism. He pointed out that after the fall of Napoleon I in 1814, the Conservative and Liberal politicians of the restoration in Europe merely opposed or modified the *results* of the Revolution, not its unbelieving *roots*.*

The final point of Kuyper's speech was that the basic antithesis between the revolutionary liberty tree and the cross of Christ concerns the nature of salvation. Kuyper sketched out the positive influence of both the Evangelical Awakening throughout Europe in the nineteenth century and the tradition of Dutch Calvinism. The evangelical movement in various countries emphasized personal repentance and the need for conversion to Christ. Evangelism, rescue missions, temperance campaigns, tract and Bible distribution, and foreign missions were undertaken. Such Christian ministry met the spiritual needs of many people who had experienced the fires of unbelief during the revolutionary period. Ethical

---

*The point that the humanist popular sovereignty ideal was the normative basis for even liberal politics had been made by Kuyper in *The Standard* as early as October 19, 1874. At that time he exposed the fallacy of the distinction made by the *New Rotterdam Daily* between the moderate affirmation of humanist autonomy in the French Constitution of 1791 and the more proletarian humanism of the Constitution of 1793. In both cases popular sovereignty was the ultimate basis of normativity. When the Rotterdam paper admitted that Dutch Liberalism was based upon the principle of the French Constitution of 1791, Kuyper declared that his basic contention had been confirmed. While Liberals disliked politics based upon street fighting and proletarian suffrage, they still were committed to the notion of autonomy which lay behind such radicalism.

liberation from the power of sin, Kuyper emphasized, could only be found in the name of Christ. Yet the evangelical movement needed the clarification of Dutch Calvinism which was specifically Reformed and concerned with all of life. It was Dr. Isaac da Costa, a converted Portuguese Jew living in Holland, who warned Christians to refrain from worshipping the secular idols of the age in the 1820s. Groen van Prinsterer became involved in politics in order to insure that the Gospel would have full freedom in church, school, and the press as well as among all social classes. Groen rightly recognized that the school was a key battleground. There the followers of Christ and the adherents of reason would fight for the allegiance of the coming generations. From small beginnings, Kuyper continued, the Anti-Revolutionary Party had grown until the Mackay Cabinet was able to take office. Now it could begin to take legal steps within a democratic context to insure that the Gospel would have unhindered influence in specific issues. Kuyper made it clear that he was a social pluralist who would continue to affirm the political rights of rationalists, Catholics, and Calvinists, even though he was also committed to church confessionalism. Thus he praised the Christian Reformed Churches of 1834 and the Reformed Churches of 1886 for separating from the modernist synod of the Dutch Reformed Church. Kuyper's political agenda called for each social group to have its rightful suffrage. He stressed the continuing importance of the free school movements, the right of labor to organize, sufficient national defense, viable international trade, the abolition of the opium trade in the Dutch East Indies, and the need to treat the Javanese as people. Support was given to the Mackay Cabinet and to the coalition of confessional parties behind it to implement Christian Democratic policies. In all of this rhetoric, Kuyper was really saying that John 3:16 is the one basic issue. It is God alone who saves His people by the merits of Christ and not by the "liberation" the politician brings. The fruit of the revolutionary liberty tree is lethal because its roots are poisoned. In conclusion, Kuyper urged his hearers to renew their commitment to the covenantal mercies: "As for us and our children we will no longer kneel before the idol of the French Revolution, but the God of our fathers will again be our God!"

"Maranatha," Kuyper's major address of 1891 explored the implications of eschatology for modern political conduct. He first asserted that belief in the visible return of the Lord Christ to the earth is the basic dividing line even for politics. Actually, his speech was a reflection on II Thessalonians 2:1-8 with emphasis on verse 8: "And then the lawless one will be revealed, and the Lord Jesus will slay him with the breath of his mouth and destroy him by his appearing and his coming." For the secular politicians—Conservative, Liberal, Radical, Marxist—belief in "Maranatha," that "the Lord is coming," is a myth to be scorned. But to us, Kuyper confessed, it is a glorious decree for the future of both our spiritual and political lives. Our opponents, he continued, refuse to recognize the royal authority of Jesus since they separate politics from religion and deny the power of the Christ of the Scriptures. But for Christians, the expectation of this "Maranatha" determines their political conduct. They are stewards of the Christ who has all power over heaven and earth. They know that human history will finally disintegrate and that God will judge the nations.

Kuyper's second theme was that the blatant spirit of secularity, flowing from the ideals of the French Revolution of 1789, is a further sign of the coming Great Apostasy. The explicitly anti-Christian spirit of secular politics in general and of Socialism in particular were becoming ever more consistently stated. The Revolution at Paris was based on a theory which honored autonomous man, not the God of the Scripture. The Bible was rejected and replaced by reason. This viewpoint says that man's destination is earthly, not heavenly. Kuyper pointed out that even Holland had been greatly influenced by this spirit of the age during the previous century. The Dutch church and the public school were subverted by humanism. Love of pleasure replaced heavenly-mindedness in the lives of many people. Marriage was discredited. Certainty was replaced by doubt (Kuyper was undoubtedly thinking of his own struggles with theological modernism at Leiden University in the early 1860s). The Liberals sought to make money, not to serve the Lord. But Kuyper also pointed out that there was a good side to the results of the Revolution. It forced Conservatives to be concerned about historical continuity; it enabled Liberals to affirm the importance of freedom, Radicals to be concerned about justice, and Socialists to be committed to public compassion. Common grace seems to be Kuyper's point here. Though there have been many manifestations of evil throughout history, it will be only at the end of the age that the anti-Christian forces will be fully visible. The struggle between Christ and satan will continue until the Prince of Peace is victorious.

The third emphasis of this speech was that Christians cannot abdicate the nation's future to the political forces committed to the humanistic spirit of the age. Christians cannot abdicate because both sin and grace are operative in public life; it is not entirely good, but it is not entirely evil either. Christians have the obligation to work for political righteousness despite the visible brokenness of society. But the task to engage in politically spiritual work is a holy calling. "The hand that grabs for personal advantage," Kuyper warned, "cannot hold the Banner of the Cross." Thus the Anti-Revolutionary delegates were urged to take part in the election campaign of 1891 with good courage. The Mackay Cabinet had only begun its work and its mandate should be renewed at the polls. But Kuyper also emphasized that one must see beyond the election to the long-term impact of Christian action. This task embraces decades and centuries. Over this long span, one must discern whether the influence of the Lord's

Name is advancing or declining. "But now we know," the chairman declared, "that even in our own fatherland, the struggle of the spirits must ultimately result in the choice: *for or against* Christ." He noted how discouraging the situation seemed when Groen van Prinsterer began articulating his politically spiritual position in the 1830s, and again in 1871 when he broke with the Christian-Conservative fusionists. Kuyper declared that Groen never dreamed that a confessional cabinet would ever take office. But while Kuyper supported the Anti-Revolutionary-Catholic governing coalition, he also pointed out that both parties must keep their independent organizations because of irreconcilable theological differences.

As he viewed European developments, Kuyper observed that the political influence of Liberal elitism was declining, while that of mass democracy and Socialism was on the rise. In this changing situation, the Anti-Revolutionary Party stood for Christian Democracy to defend the rights of the Protestant common folk. In this period of flux Kuyper encouraged the party to work for the following: (1) the honoring of the religio-ethical concerns of the nation above purely material well-being; (2) the full re-establishment of freedom of conscience for both the rich and poor by opposing governmental interference in spiritual matters such as education; (3) the introduction of an electoral system of proportional representation; and (4) the encouragement of public compassion by the passage of legislation to help the poor as well as the rich. Kuyper ended by urging that the Anti-Revolutionary delegates go forward in the name of the Lord.

Conclusions

1. In these two speeches we see a remarkable unity between the visions of the temporal and of the eternal. The relationship between, on the one hand, the tasks of the Anti-Revolutionary Party and the Mackay Cabinet,

and, on the other hand, Christian witness throughout the centuries, culminating in the ultimate victory of Christ, is presented in a masterful way. Kuyper clearly emphasized how decisive salvation and the Lord's return are for our lives on earth as well as in heaven. We see in this presentation a glorious defense of the faith and an amazingly relevant preaching of the Gospel. How great is the comfort of the Scriptures presented here!

2. Kuyper's amillennialism enabled him to engage in political action. He recognized the biblical truth that both sin and grace are operative in history (Matthew 13:24-30). His position was neither totally pessimistic and negative nor totally optimistic. Kuyper's realistic position allowed Christian social concern to be expressed as defense, as witness, and as an alternative between the cross and the Second Coming.

Kuyper as a Member of Parliament in about 1898 (Documentatiecentrum, Vrije Universiteit te Amsterdam courtesy of its director, Dr. George Puchinger).

Chapter 6

The Perils of Democratic Progress

THE 1890S WERE A TIME of great tension and change for the Anti-Revolutionary Party and Dutch society. The movement for mass democracy and against social elitism embraced supporters from diverse political and social movements. In 1891 the first Christian Social Congress was held in Amsterdam. Dr. Abraham Kuyper delivered his prophetic address on *Christianity and the Class Struggle*. Speaking of the plight of the disenfranchised masses he declared, ". . . The social question has become *the* question, the burning life-question, of the end of the nineteenth century." It is indeed a blessing to have this magnificent Christian manifesto in English. Kuyper recognized that the problem of poverty was a spiritual, social, and political problem requiring the active support of Christian reformists to properly emancipate the lower classes. His commitment to such reform was one of the main characteristics of his public activities during this transitional phase of his career. Quite early, he recognized that poverty was a serious problem, and wrote a series of important articles on the issue in *The Standard* during the spring of 1872.

The Tak Cabinet

In August 1891 the Liberal Tak van Poortvliet Cabinet came into power, determined to bring about

49

social reform. This Cabinet was supported by the Left majority comprised of 54 Liberals and one Radical. The Right minority of 45 embraced 20 Anti-Revolutionaries and 25 Catholics. The executive committee of the Liberal Union Party endorsed J.P.R. Tak van Poortvliet's goal of working for universal suffrage. As Minister of Internal Affairs, Tak wanted a suffrage bill passed that would enfranchise everyone who could read, write and support himself. But such a proposal was questioned by many; in fact, the Dutch constitution made additional requirements for widening the vote. The controversy surrounding Tak's proposal caused the fall of his cabinet due to internal disagreements. There were also splits in both the Liberal Union and the Anti-Revolutionary Parties in early 1894. The less progressive group, following the Liberal parliamentarians W.H. de Beaufort and S. van Houten, separated from the Liberal Union Party and called themselves Old Liberals. In 1906 they finally formed the League of Free Liberals. A similar series of events took place within the Anti-Revolutionary Party. Party chairman Kuyper and parliamentarian Theodorus Heemskerk supported Tak's proposal while other parliamentarians, most notably Jonkheer Alexander F. de Savornin Lohman and Baron Aeneas Mackay, opposed it. A split occurred, and the Lohman group called itself the Free Anti-Revolutionary Party. Between 1903 and 1908 the Lohman group became a main part of the Christian Historical Union. It is interesting to note that there was no split in the Catholic Party. The Catholic leader, Mgr. Herman Schaepman, supported Tak's proposal.

Christian Democracy vs. Conservatism

On March 30, 1894, Dr. Abraham Kuyper addressed the special congress of his party held at Utrecht in preparation for the coming election. *The Standard* covered these party congresses as a matter of course since it was the leading Anti-Revolutionary daily newspaper.

Kuyper began with prayer and a few words of appreciation for the Christian political witness of L.W.C. Keuchenius and Jonkheer P.J. Elout van Soeterwoude, who had both recently died. Both men had represented the party's cause in Parliament and the former had also served as Minister of Colonies in the Mackay Cabinet from 1888 to 1890.

Kuyper then addressed himself to the question of the rise of the democratic mass movement in the Netherlands. He pointed out that in *The Herald* weekly as early as November 5, 1869 and in *The Standard* on June 5, 1873, he had called for a widening of the vote in order that democracy might protect the rights of the powerless common people of the lower middle class. All social classes should be able to influence public policy through voting. Our calling, he declared, is to develop a Christian Democratic movement to bring justice to the "People behind the Voters" (to use Groen van Prinsterer's phrase). Such a movement would help Christians as well as others. "Equal Rights for All!" was Kuyper's slogan. He reiterated Groen's approval of this Christian Democratic struggle for political emancipation from the control of the unbelieving financial elite. Concern with the unenfranchised masses was very important since the Socialists were also seeking to woo the lower classes. The people must recognize the vital character of obedience to God's law understood from the perspective of historic Calvinism. Such understanding, Kuyper asserted, is essential to the nation's future. We do not seek the worker's paradise of the Socialists, he added, but rather, the revitalization of the historic Protestant traditions of the people. Therefore he had rejoiced when the suffrage reform bill of Minister Tak van Poortvliet was presented to Parliament. The upcoming election would give a definitive answer to this important matter. Reference was also made to the severing of ties between the party's Central Committee and its parliamentary caucus.

When Kuyper finished his remarks, four resolutions were passed.

1. The party congress unanimously expressed its thanks to God for Kuyper's quarter-century of leadership as chairman and prayed that the Lord would continue to give him wisdom as a further blessing to church, school, crown and fatherland. (Such a re-affirmation of Kuyper's leadership was felt to be necessary after the split in the party and the exodus of the Lohman group. Kuyper had encouraged them to leave.)

2. Thanks were expressed to the Regent, Queen Emma, for calling for new elections when the suffrage reform bill had not been passed, which had caused a governmental crisis.

3. The party congress expressed the conviction that the coming election was a struggle between those favoring various shades of conservatism and those who defended "The People Behind the Voters." The Anti-Revolutionary Party went on record as opposed to such conservatism.

4. The Congress declared it to be in the national interest to work at once for a final extension of the suffrage to the constitutionally prescribed limits.

Armed with such resolutions, the Anti-Revolutionary Party prepared for the coming political contest.

"For or Against Tak" was the key issue of the election of 1894. The majority of 56 elected to Parliament were anti-Takians while the minority of 44 were Takians. The suffrage question cut across party lines. One Takian newly elected was Dr. Kuyper himself, who represented the Sliedrecht district (near Dordrecht). In addition to being party chairman, Kuyper now became the leader of the Anti-Revolutionary parliamentary caucus. Another caucus was formed around Lohman. In 1895, after Kuyper publicly criticized Lohman's legal views, Lohman resigned his post as Professor of Law at the Free University of Amsterdam. The split in the Anti-Revolutionary Party was, unfortunately, a painful reality.

Van Houten Suffrage Reform Bill

After the 1894 election, the anti-Takian Roell-Van Houten Cabinet made up exclusively of Old Liberals, took power. As Minister of Internal Affairs, S. Van Houten introduced a suffrage reform bill to Parliament in early 1896. While avoiding the universalism of Tak's unsuccessful bill, Van Houten did want to widen the vote significantly by specifying a lesser amount of taxes a person paid than previous proposals had specified. Thus the principle of relating the right to vote to a man's income and tax rate was maintained. Van Houten also proposed that a person could become a political candidate by gathering only forty signatures and that the use of the secret ballot be guaranteed.

Kuyper, as leader of his Anti-Revolutionary caucus, took part in the parliamentary debate on the Van Houten Suffrage Reform Bill on May 13 and 20, 1896. Two major themes can be discerned in his remarks: (1) he objected to this bill because of the humanistic principle undergirding it, and (2) he presented an alternative proposal on the question. Concerning the first theme, widening the vote was not the issue for Kuyper. His concern was the basis on which suffrage reform would be realized. The Van Houten Bill was unacceptable to Kuyper because it was based on the humanistic principle that income alone determined enfranchisement. Kuyper feared that big businessmen would deliberately keep salaries low to prevent their workers from voting. If passed, this bill based upon income would frustrate many workers in such urban centers as Rotterdam and Amsterdam, for only an "aristocracy of workers" would be given the vote. The bill was based on a "false democracy" that denied subjection to the ordinances of God and opened the way to greater political relativism.

To make his point more concretely, Kuyper read a resolution of the Calvinist labor association: "The Netherlandic Labor Union Patrimonium since its most recent annual conference has been disappointed in its hope that franchise reform would be separated from even a disguised tax on income. Patrimonium regrets that in the pending (Van Houten) bill, the above-named tie (between franchise and income) will be maintained, thus depriving thousands of workers unjustly of the right to vote."

This bill, Kuyper emphasized, was too progressive for the *status-quo* politician yet too conservative for the nation. He freely acknowledged that his own party was comprised of commoners (kleine luiden), many of whom were still the "People Behind the Voters." He was fighting for proper suffrage reform for them and others. He spoke frankly about the splits in the Anti-Revolutionary and Liberal Union Parties between the conservatives and the progressives on this issue. But Kuyper hotly denied the charge by the Free Anti-Revolutionary parliamentarian, Jonkheer G.J. Th. Beerlaerts van Blokland, that he (Kuyper) had joined the progressive wing of the humanist Liberal Union Party.

Kuyper's alternative to the Van Houten bill, his second theme, emphasized the two-fold sovereignty delegated by God to both government and people. Each grouping, represented by cabinet and Parliament, has its own responsibility to bring justice and harmony to the nation. Kuyper distinguished the task of Crown and cabinet from the task of the legislature. He rejected popular sovereignty out of hand due to its presupposition of human autonomy, but he did recognize that the vote could legitimately be extended to all citizens in a specific country. Householder suffrage, based on the representation of families, not individuals, was Kuyper's alternative proposal. A revision of the constitution would be required in order for Anti-Revolutionary principles to be applied to this question. Ultimately, the member from Sliedrecht said, he wanted a bill that would relate the suffrage issue to spiritual and human aspects of citizenship and not just to a monetary requirement. Kuyper made it clear that he favored widening the vote but was opposed to the Van Houten bill.

After all the debates were finished and the parliamentary votes taken, the Van Houten Suffrage Reform Bill was passed into law. The number of Dutch voters was doubled from 300,000 to 600,000. Mass democracy took a giant step forward in an orderly fashion.

Afterthoughts

1. Something about Kuyper the politician can be learned from his voting against the Suffrage Reform Act in 1896. We should also note that he voted against the Child Labor Law proposed by the same Van Houten in 1874 during Kuyper's first term in Parliament. He did favor reforms both to protect children from labor exploitation and to widen the vote. But he disapproved of the humanistic principles underlying these bills and so he voted against them. Undoubtedly, he knew that both would pass in spite of his negative votes. He supported both his Christian principles and his reformist concerns, yet without having to compromise his principles with favorable votes for these bills. We could say Kuyper had his cake and ate it too.

2. Kuyper correctly sensed that the movement for a mass democracy was a legitimate concern of the political parties and the people. He also recognized that suffrage reform would help greatly to emancipate the Reformed commoners (as well as other groups of ordinary folk) and thus strengthen the Anti-Revolutionary Party's national influence. Since this suffrage reform movement was a matter of public justice, Kuyper had the courage to oppose the more conservative and aristocratic elements within his own party. The resulting split is to be lamented, but it was probably inevitable. The history of the Anti-Revolutionary Party has been a stormy one indeed.

3. Kuyper desired to give a Christian Democratic

basis to this mass movement. He did not want people to think that this question was the sole property of Liberals and Socialists. Thus he wanted a suffrage reform bill that would give credence even to the non-material aspects of the citizenship question. His conviction was made clear: the normativity of God's law is applicable to the people, and they can legitimately exercise an aspect of divine sovereignty through the Parliament which is independent from the Crown and government. Again, Kuyper's political instincts were biblical and progressive in a responsible way.

Kuyper at Princeton Theological Seminary in New Jersey where he delivered his *Lectures on Calvinism* in 1898 (Documentatiecentrum, Vrije
Universiteit te Amsterdam courtesy of its director, Dr. George Puchinger).

Chapter 7

Prelude to Power

" **W**E STAND AT THE THRESHOLD of a new period in the life of our country. With the Van Houten Suffrage Reform Act of 1896, the extension of the vote to all social classes to complete the democratic process is only a matter of time. The political power of the old elite has been broken. As it completes its twenty-year struggle for suffrage reform, the Anti-Revolutionary Party extends its warmest greetings to the new voters. Our nation must now turn its attention to the social question."

With this powerful statement affirming democratic reform, Dr. Abraham Kuyper opened the election campaign of the Anti-Revolutionary Party on April 29, 1897 in Utrecht. As both the party's national chairman and its parliamentary leader, Kuyper looked to the coming election campaign with great anticipation. *The Standard* Christian daily newspaper gave two days of coverage to this Congress in its columns.

The Election of 1897

Kuyper's address was brief but powerful. He urged the party delegates to maintain Calvinistic principles and party independence in this new period. The ordinances of God have relevance in all of life including its personal,

familial, and national aspects. Everything should be done
to the glory of God. The Holy Scriptures, Kuyper affirmed, are normative even for our political reflection. He
warned against watering down this biblical authority with
such terms as "Gospel" or "the principles of the Gospel"
when such terms were filled with revolutionary content.
Terms could be either used properly or abused. Undoubtedly he was referring here to the early phase of a
"Christians for Socialism/Marxism" movement. The
Anti-Revolutionary Party stood on the full authority of
Scripture. Affirming the antithesis of Christianity versus
humanism, it rejected any denial or relativizing of that
authority.

Kuyper then spoke of his Calvinist approach to the
question of poverty, his alternative to both Conservative
elitism on the Right and Socialism on the Left. A Christian Democratic mass movement could be a key to dealing
with this social question. He warned against unlimited
free enterprise which made an idol of profits and con-
sumption. The party, Kuyper declared, will seek to help
the weak so that they will be psychologically able to stand
on their own feet. The Christian principle also required
that a proper balance between city and countryside be
realized.

Kuyper also strongly criticized the centralizing plans
of the Social Democrats. They wanted the state to control
all of society, eliminating the various free social spheres.
Kuyper affirmed his belief in the proper use of private
property within a constitutional context. Private initiative
and sphere sovereignty were concepts to be used to help
the lower classes improve themselves. Kuyper pointed out
that the Christian position was a rejection of both the idol
of a capitalist Mammon on the Right and the idol of the
Socialist Redeemer State on the Left. He saw both free
enterprise and the task of the state as normed by the
Biblical ordinances of God: man as a sinner, the validity
of the Ten Commandments for individuals and states,
private enterprise as stewardship and the task of the state

to promulgate public justice. Thus he stated, ". . . for us a religious, historic and national political party, there can be no solution to the social question until the common man in the cities and the farmers in the rural areas are again assured of having their own places in the organic national system." The social dislocations and shocks caused by overpopulation, factory exploitation and rural poverty had to be overcome. Kuyper obviously felt that the political and social emancipation of the common man was the way to restore this balance.

Regret was expressed that the aristocratic group around Jonkheer Alexander F. de Savornin Lohman had separated itself from the party several years earlier. Kuyper expressed his appreciation for these Free Anti-Revolutionaries who had earlier made an important contribution to the party. There was space in the party for both Christian aristocrats and Christian commoners. But the Lohman group refused to stay in the party. Kuyper appealed, "Brothers, come back to us!" However, full reconciliation was impossible because Lohman felt Kuyper was not always honest.

Near the end of the speech, Kuyper referred to the position of the Anti-Revolutionary Party in relation to the Old Liberal, progressive Union Liberal, and Catholic movements. He saw little long-term significance in the *status quo* position of the Old Liberals; however, as he pointed out, his party shared with the Catholics the conviction that Christianity had relevance for public affairs. The Anti-Revolutionary Party likewise shared with the progressive Union Liberals a concern for freedom of thought and personal liberties. Kuyper then brilliantly declared:

> Due to our principle and tradition, we will stand with the Catholics for the Christian concerns against the progressive Liberals and with the progressives for personal freedoms against the Catholics . . . We Anti-Revolutionaries have the task of standing for both the Christian religion and liberty in an integrated fashion.

With these words, the delegates were urged to wage the parliamentary election campaign with God's weapons of persuasion, love and toleration.

When the election took place a few weeks later, the Left won 55 parliamentary seats and the Right 45. The Left majority included 33 Union Liberals, 15 Old Liberals, 4 Radicals, 2 Social Democrats and one free Socialist. The most important of these newly elected Socialists was the Frisian lawyer P.J. Troelstra who was the main founder of the Social Democratic Worker's Party in 1894. Troelstra's party was frankly Marxist in affirming the class struggle and calling for the nationalization of all industries. Yet unlike the more anti-parliamentary Marxist groups, it agreed to take part in democratic politics. The election also marked the last time that there would be a Liberal parliamentary majority.

The 45 seats on the Right were held by 22 Catholics, 17 Anti-Revolutionaries, 5 Free Anti-Revolutionaries and one Christian Historical. As his party's parliamentary leader, Kuyper was himself re-elected to the Second Chamber.

The Pierson Cabinet

Since the Liberals were the majority, the moderate Union Liberal leader N.G. Pierson became the new Prime Minister and also served as Minister of Finance. Some of the other Cabinet ministers were: H. Goeman Borgesius (Union Liberal, Internal Affairs), W.H. de Beaufort (Old Liberal, Foreign Affairs), P.W.A. Cort van der Linden (Union Liberal, Justice), and Dr. C. Lely (Union Liberal, Water Works, Trade and Industry). The Pierson Cabinet was announced as a social justice ministry. A series of reform bills were prepared by Prime Minister Pierson and his ministerial colleagues during the next few months.

On December 1, 1897 party leader Kuyper entered the debate on cabinet policy in the parliamentary Binnenhof in The Hague. He sought to express the Anti-

Revolutionary viewpoint towards the new government. As was his custom since 1872, Kuyper attempted to ask questions of a cabinet that would cause it to clarify its own position. Such clarity would make it easier for the Anti-Revolutionary leader to either criticize or support a government.

Kuyper began his remarks by noting that four new parties were represented for the first time in Parliament: the Social Democratic Workers' Party, the Christian Historical Party and the Free Anti-Revolutionary Party of Lohman. He was aware of the changes represented by these new groups.

At the outset, Kuyper stated that the Anti-Revolutionary Party was part of Her Majesty's Loyal Opposition. At the same time he expressed his high regard for the cabinet ministers. He hoped to cooperate with the government to the extent permitted by his principles. He quoted the writings of the Liberal professor J.T. Buys and the late Anti-Revolutionary leader Groen van Prinsterer to the effect that in order to be effective, a cabinet should be unified in terms of its composition and political agenda. In a number of different ways Kuyper asked Prime Minister Pierson if his cabinet was indeed unified. The Anti-Revolutionary leader then declared that Pierson would have to deal with several important matters including the coming inauguration of Queen Wilhelmina, the unification of the divided Liberal forces, the necessary reform bills and certain financial matters.

Concerning the inauguration, Kuyper noted a clash between popular sovereignty and royal sovereignty. He quoted Justice Minister Cort van der Linden as making a statement to the effect that a government rules by the will of the people alone and not by the grace of God. The popular sovereignty view meant that Wilhelmina would become Queen and thus the bearer of national sovereignty through the will of the people. Kuyper's view was that Wilhelmina became the sovereign Queen in her own right as the heir of the House of Orange. What was the cabinet's viewpoint on this question? Kuyper asked.

Kuyper recognized Prime Minister Pierson, the moderate Union Liberal, as most able to unify the divided Liberal factions. Kuyper pointed out that during the recent campaign, Liberals such as Cort van den Linden were guilty of labeling anyone who believed the Bible as normative for society as "clerical." Kuyper objected to this "clerical" charge as a misrepresentation of his own Protestant party. He urged the Cabinet to get beyond negative slogans like "anti-clerical" and to take a firm, positive position. Kuyper noted De Beaufort's assertion of a difference in principle between Liberals on the one hand and Socialists and Radicals on the other, and Goeman Borgesius' assertion that progressive Liberals and Radicals were agreed on the principle that more government involvement was needed to lessen the gulf between the poor and the rich. Kuyper expressed his own view, echoing Groen, that the Conservative (Old Liberal) stands today where the Liberal stood yesterday; the Liberal will stand the day after tomorrow where the Radical is today. Kuyper's point was that all secular parties, based on Enlightenment humanism, differ only in tempo while sharing a common belief in human autonomy. Is there unity in the Liberal composition of the cabinet? Kuyper wondered.

Since the Pierson government was a social reform cabinet Kuyper declared his party's willingness to contribute to social reform legislation. But he pointed out the differences between the individualistic *laissez faire* school and the socially-oriented ethical school of thought on economic matters. The Anti-Revolutionary Party rejected the old *laissez faire* economic views, and affirmed a critical acceptance of the new socially-oriented view. But this critical acceptance, Kuyper emphasized, involved the use of principles based upon biblical normativity. He stressed the biblical notion of man's stewardship over the creation. The Christian world-view opposed the humanist world-view on this matter. The ownership of private property was normed by the principle of stewardship and not by humanist speculations based on reason and evolutionary development. Kuyper wanted to see the principle of stewardship incorporated in social reform laws. What, Kuyper asked in conclusion, would cause the cabinet to speak clearly on the basis for social reforms?

On the following day, December 2, 1897, Kuyper again addressed his parliamentary colleagues. He hotly denied the charge that many Anti-Revolutionaries, in their zeal to promote popular reforms that others of their persuasion rejected, had in practice joined a mass secular democratic party. He reaffirmed the difference in principle between Christian and humanistic parties. Such a charge probably came from Old Liberals and the Lohman group that opposed these democratic reforms. Kuyper firmly exclaimed, "The Christian principle which is the source of my convictions, my confession, and even my politics, I will maintain even as a democrat."

The charge was made by the Left Union Liberal parliamentarian, A. Kerdijk, that the Anti-Revolutionary leader was concerned only with the non-material aspects of social reform, while the Liberals thought only about the material interests of such matters. Kuyper responded by acknowledging a basic difference in outlook of the two parties, but he asserted that his party was concerned about both aspects of the social problem. Thus cooperation was possible. Reform laws to deal with concrete material problems of poverty could be framed in spite of different world-view perspectives. Having made his point, Kuyper returned to his seat.

The Worker's Social Insurance Bill, introduced by Minister Lely in 1899, was one of the Pierson Cabinet's most important legislative proposals. It proposed to provide financial protection for workers hurt on the job and to be funded either by the Royal Insurance Bank, by private insurance companies, or by employers themselves. Kuyper spoke extensively on this matter in the parliamentary debates during October and November, 1899, and in

October, 1900. The Worker's Social Insurance Act of 1901 was the first piece of social legislation to protect workers in the nation's history, and Kuyper's contribution to it was significant.

The inauguration of the youthful Queen Wilhelmina took place on September 6, 1898, and the Regency of her mother, Queen Emma, came to a close. Queen Wilhelmina married Duke Henry of Mecklenburg Schwerin during February, 1901, and he officially became Prince Henry of the Netherlands.

The Grand Coalition

As the election contest of 1901 approached, Kuyper gave his address, "Keep Faith with Our Ideal," to the party congress of April 17, 1901 in Utrecht. Reports were carried in *The Standard* on April 18 and 19.

The disunity of the Pierson Cabinet was Kuyper's first theme. The artificial Liberal majority of Old Liberals, progressives, Radicals and even Social Democrats was breaking up. Disagreements within the government and Parliament about cabinet policy had weakened Prime Minister Pierson's position.

The prospects for the post-election regrouping was Kuyper's second theme. While Kuyper recognized that the Anti-Revolutionary Party would not gain a parliamentary majority for a Cabinet of its own, he did believe that his party could win at least 25 seats. We do not fight for cabinet portfolios, he declared, but we seek to strengthen the ethical bonds between the Dutch electorate and God. It was entirely within the realm of possibility that the Christian parties together would win a parliamentary majority. The Party delegates were urged to keep their faith in the Calvinistic ideals, for great perseverance would be needed in the coming campaign.

Recognition of the Catholic contribution to Christian politics was Kuyper's third theme. He spoke of Groen's appreciation for the writings of the French priest Felicité de Lamennais, the German professor K.L. von

Haller and the French political thinker, the Viscount L.G.A. de Bonald. These Catholic critiques of secular and revolutionary politics were of continuing importance. Kuyper pointed out honestly that the Anti-Revolution was broader than just Reformed groups; it also included Catholics. In a very important statement, Kuyper expressed his conviction that Dutch Catholics were committed to full toleration and democracy. A general political coalition between Anti-Revolutionaries and Catholics could prevent the continued dominance of the secular parties. Kuyper emphasized that this should be a coalition of independent parties, ruling out the prospect of the union of churches or of political parties.

The fourth and final theme of the speech concerned potential dangers to the Anti-Revolutionary Party in the coming election: engaging in ivory tower discussions while carelessly ignoring practical work, and being tempted to play dirty politics. Kuyper urged the delegates to engage in responsible activism, to pray about the results of the campaign, and to expect the Lord to give spiritual strength so that a more dynamic Christian presence in national politics might be realized.

Reflections

1. Kuyper correctly sensed the historic importance of the change in politics from political elitism to mass democracy. He wanted to use the democratic movement to strengthen the Christian social influence legitimately, as it developed within a national pluralistic framework. In his frank engagement with the social question of poverty, Kuyper would not allow the Socialists to shout arrogantly that they alone were concerned about the plight of the lower classes. In relation to the rise of mass democracy and social concern, the Anti-Revolutionary Party was able to reveal its true nature as an emancipation movement. In his concern to integrate Christian normativity with social liberty, Kuyper sought to organize a politics of stewardship. His position was neither Conser-

vative, Liberal, nor Socialist, but Christian Democratic.

2. We see in the 1901 speech, "Keep Faith with Our Ideal," a further refinement of the grand coalition between Anti-Revolutionaries and Catholics that dominated Dutch governments for decades even up to the Van Agt Cabinet which took office in 1977. Kuyper and Mgr. Herman Schaepman, the leader of the Catholic Party, were the architects of this grand coalition. Under Mgr. Schaepman's leadership, the Catholic Party members held to an orthodox Catholicism with which Anti-Revolutionaries could find practical agreement. With this political coalition in the process of formation, Kuyper saw the possibility of a second Christian coalition cabinet, and he prepared his party for it. But with all of his practical cooperation with the Catholic Party, Kuyper made clear to all the unbridgeable gap between the theology of Calvinism and that of Rome. This recognition of differences made political cooperation on specific issues possible. The emergence of the grand coalition was indeed Kuyper's prelude to power, for he himself became Prime Minister of the Netherlands during the summer of 1901.

Kuyper in Power

1901-1905

Prime Minister Kuyper (marked by the "X") listens while Queen Wilhelmina reads the annual Speech from the Throne outlining his governmental program at the opening of the States-General or Parliament in The Hague (Documentatiecentrum, Vrije Universiteit te Amsterdam courtesy of its director, Dr. George Puchinger).

Chapter 8

Prime Minister
in 1901

" *T* HE PARTIES OF THE PARLIAMENTARY Left and
Right, in my opinion, are agreed that they seek to
apply in all legislation the ordinance: 'Thou shalt love thy
neighbor as thyself.' But the parties of the Right, in
distinction from the parliamentary groupings of the Left,
accept the additional word from Him who spoke the first
word: 'Thou shalt love the Lord thy God with all thy
mind and strength. This is the first and the great com-
mandment.'

"Every member of the parties of the Right bows
before these words and I also hasten to add that every
member of the cabinet does likewise with full respect."

This impressive confession of faith was made on
December 5, 1901, by Prime Minister Abraham Kuyper
during a parliamentary debate taking place within a few
months of his assumption of governmental power. Dr.
Kuyper was determined to apply Christian principles to
state policy even as he spoke from behind the governmental Green Table in the Second Chamber of the Parliament in The Hague.

The Preparation

Kuyper had prepared the Anti-Revolutionary constituency for the possibility of a confessional cabinet in his party congress address entitled "Keep Faith with Our Ideal" delivered in Utrecht on April 17, 1901. The party then campaigned on a platform calling for (1) a final solution to the education problem within the bounds of the Dutch constitution; (2) the implementation of an obligatory insurance program for the sick, the elderly and invalids to be financed by the state; and (3) the funding of this insurance program by a judicious raising of import duties that would likewise improve the national labor situation.

National parliamentary elections were held in June. On the Right, the Anti-Revolutionaries won 24 seats, the Free Anti-Revolutionaries (under the leadership of Jonkheer A.F. de Savornin Lohman) won 7, the Roman Catholics (under Mgr. Herman Schaepman) received 25 and the Christian Historicals had 2. On the Left, the recent splits within Liberalism were painfully visible. Since the Liberal Union Party had become a *status quo* party, some progressives in March, 1901, had split from it to form the Liberal Democratic Alliance. This new party was dedicated to working for universal suffrage for men and women as well as for social legislation to eliminate the institutional causes of inequality. A group of independent-minded Free Liberals formed yet another split-off faction. The Liberal Union Party won 18 seats, the Liberal Democratic Alliance, 9, the Free Liberals, 8, and the Socialists, 7. Thus out of a total of 100 seats in the Second Chamber, the parties of the Right won 58 seats while those of the Left received only 42.

Of the two major confessional parties, Mgr. Schaepman was the leader of the Catholic Party's caucus and Kuyper chaired the Anti-Revolutionary caucus. Queen Wilhelmina appointed Kuyper as Prime Minister-designate with responsibility for forming the new cabinet. At this point Kuyper resigned his theological professorship at the Free University of Amsterdam and his chairmanship of the central committee of his own party. He also stopped writing editorials for *The Standard* daily newspaper.

The First Months in Power

The Kuyper administration took power on August 1, 1901. Kuyper served as Prime Minister and Minister of Internal Affairs. The other members of the cabinet were J.C. de Marez Oyens (Waterworks, Trade and Industry, Anti-Revolutionary), Jonkheer T.A.J. Van Asch van Wyck (Colonies, Anti-Revolutionary; at his death in 1902 he was replaced by a party colleague, A.W.F. Idenburg), J.A. Loeff (Justice, Catholic), J.W. Bergansius (War, Catholic), J.J.I. Harte van Tecklenburg (Finances, Catholic), Baron R. Melvil van Lynden (Foreign Affairs, non-party) and G. Kruys (Navy, non-party; at his death he was temporarily replaced by J.W. Bergansius and then by A.G. Ellis). Thus the cabinet was composed of members of the two major confessional parties and included several non-party ministers. (Both the Free Anti-Revolutionaries of Lohman and the Christian Historicals declined to join the cabinet.) There was rejoicing in the confessional parties but especially among Anti-Revolutionaries. Kuyper was the only opposition journalist who ever became Prime Minister of the Netherlands. At last a Reformed commoner, the spokesman of the Anti-Revolutionary *kleine luiden*, was in power!

On September 17, Queen Wilhelmina opened Parliament with the annual Speech from the Throne, written by the Prime Minister, as always. Emphasizing the spiritual interests of the nation, the Queen declared that cabinet policy would be built on the Christian foundations of society. The ethical character of public life would have to be more carefully protected by law. The Queen also noted that the cabinet planned to complete the liberation of education and to introduce various social reform bills. In the Netherlands East Indies, the Queen continued, the government had the obligation to protect the rights of inland Christians, to give more support for Christian missions and to see that administrative policy was permeated by the intention of government to carry out an ethical colonial policy.

First Major Statement

During the summer and fall of 1901 certain tensions had been built up in Parliament as to the true nature and intentions of the new cabinet. In the years since the beginning of his political career in 1872, Kuyper had not only won a following of Reformed commoners but he had also gained many enemies due to his relentless attacks in *The Standard* on his opponents, especially the Liberals. As a major opposition journalist, for almost thirty years Kuyper had been attacking the Liberal establishment which held national political power. Thus when his own government was formed, the parties of the parliamentary Left were understandably suspicious of his leadership. Many wondered if he would really carry out the promised democratic reforms on a pluralist basis or engage in theocratic repression of his enemies.

At the beginning of December, the Prime Minister issued a note of clarification to Parliament. This note was a helpful articulation of the cabinet's Christian position then under attack by the opposition.

In this written document, Kuyper affirmed that there are two types of Christian principles: (1) theological principles in a more exclusive sense that deal with the doctrine of salvation and (2), political principles related to Christian norms for public affairs. This second type of Christian principle, affirming the necessary religious basis for public conduct, would be the concern of the Prime Minister and his cabinet. While the Christian political and social principles were related to theological concepts, they had a special place in the common grace aspect of life. The Prime Minister pointed out that while it was true that there were many self-confessed Christians even in secular parties, the controversy surrounding Christian political principles concerned the validity or irrelevance of God's Law and His normative authority for public life. In the Prime Minister's view, divine revelation has a definite bearing on state policy. He also expressed appreciation for the Christian Democratic parties which, unlike the class parties of the parliamentary Right and Left, embraced members from both the higher and lower classes.

Kuyper's document described his cabinet as a government of coalition between the two major confessional parties. The Anti-Revolutionary and Catholic parties were fully independent organizations; at the same time they were in general agreement on the relation of religious faith to statecraft. Above all, both parties had signed a common political program on the objectives of the new cabinet. The Prime Minister added that such a coalition did not compromise the distinctive characteristics of either the Catholic or the Protestant party. With the final decline of Liberalism as a majority party, Kuyper saw such multi-party coalition cabinets as the wave of the present and the future. While expressing his appreciation for the work of the confessional parties as well as for aspects of Liberalism's contribution to the passage of various public laws, the Prime Minister announced that the cabinet would seek first the righteousness of God, expecting that God's blessings would be given unto them. He then listed some of the bills his government was introducing for parliamentary consideration—a proposal to curb drunkenness, continued reform of primary education, insurance law revision, health insurance, upward revision of customs duties, public health codes for housing, improved street safety and a personal taxation bill. The Prime Minister ended his note by defending his policy of Dutch neutrality towards the war in South Africa between the British and the Boers.

Behind the Green Table

The Prime Minister then spent three days, December 4 to 6, clarifying his position further. He began by commenting with a smile that he had been a journalist for 30 years and had 127 publications to his credit but it was only now that members of the parties of the Left were reading his publications including theological works such as his book on the Sabbath! But Kuyper emphasized that he spoke not as a theologian but as a statesman.

Parliament was debating the relationship of belief or unbelief to politics, and especially to cabinet policy. The head of government used this opportunity to speak about reason and revelation. It seemed that a member of the Opposition was trying to drive a wedge between the Anti-Revolutionaries and the Catholics by suggesting that for Protestants reason was useless. Kuyper quoted Calvin to the effect that reason cannot lead to saving knowledge of God but that it does have a common grace function in relation to natural life. Kuyper admitted that believers disagreed as to the function of reason, but then he quickly pointed out that among humanistic rationalists, there were some twenty different definitions of reason. The clear implication was that the Opposition could not self-righteously criticize the cabinet for being a coalition government with some basic disagreements among themselves when the Opposition was divided among itself about "rational" policy suggestions.

On the following day the Prime Minister reaffirmed that his Christian political position was democratic, not theocratic. "We do not examine anyone's faith," he said reassuringly, "nor act as heresy-hunters seeking to prove the unbelief of our fellow citizens. For us the only question is this: Who stands with us in upholding a common political conviction on the basis of Scripture?" On this basis, according to the Anti-Revolutionary viewpoint, the party offered a general program of pluralist reform for the entire country. Kuyper added that his government sought to serve the national interest, not the concerns of one party. He acknowledged the three major groups in Parliament: Christian Democrats, Liberal Democrats and Social Democrats. The Prime Minister stated that he was a Christian Democrat. However, the notion that his politics should be conducted on the basis of a "Christianity above dogma" was false because non-doctrinal Christianity is not Christianity. He preferred to speak of "Christianity below dogma." Catholics and Calvinists could work together while maintaining all of their distinctions because their cooperation took place in the common grace political arena. Their theological and ecclesiastical differences were not the subject of political discussion.

As the Prime Minister looked around the Chamber from behind the Green Table, he felt very grateful for the support given to his cabinet. He warmly thanked the confessional parties for their support, especially Jonkheer A.F. de Savornin Lohman and Mgr. Herman Schaepman. He hoped the parties on the Right side of the Chamber could cooperate as a working majority. The parties of the Left were also thanked for forming the Loyal Opposition. But Kuyper couldn't resist telling why he had called them "Liberalists" all these years. He had always used this term to indicate his conviction that they were more elitist than truly liberal. The Prime Minister concluded by reaffirming the Christian Democratic position of his cabinet, recognizing the support of the parliamentary Right and appealing to the Opposition for constructive suggestions. Kuyper then left the Green Table to return to the Prime Minister's office.

Conclusions

1. Kuyper's references to the parliamentary Left and Right should not be taken as a sign that he accepted the Conservative-Liberal-Socialist frame of reference of humanist politics. The Prime Minster used the terms "Left" and "Right" in reference to the seating ar-

rangements of law-makers in the parliamentary Second
Chamber. On a deeper level, as a Groenian, Kuyper
believed that accepting or denying the Gospel's implications for public life was the basic antithesis, not
Left/Right. That is why his governing coalition was composed of the two major confessional parties and was not
an alliance with secular moderates.

2. Kuyper's first statements as Prime Minister in
1901 reaffirmed his faith in democratic pluralism and
social reform on a Christian Democratic basis. He wisely
spoke to quiet fears that he might engage in theocratic
repression of non-Christians. Such fears of theocracy, a
legacy of medieval times, surface whenever an Evangelical
Christian becomes the chief executive of a government.
Such fears were even expressed during the American
presidential campaign in 1976. In power, President
Jimmy Carter, like Abraham Kuyper, had to make clear
his commitment to pluralism and democratic reform.

3. Kuyper's assumption of power was an example of
the paradox of partisanship. Assuming a partisan position
and accepting the partisanships of others can open the
way for public impartiality. Mutual respect for differences in a pluralist framework can result in governmental cooperation, and the creation of a climate of trust
and political stability.

The reflective Protestant Christian Democrat (Documentatiecentrum, Vrije Universiteit te Amsterdam courtesy of its director, Dr. George Puchinger).

Chapter 9

Cabinet Policy
in 1902

"*I* WILL NOW DEAL WITH THE CHARGE that this cabinet is a do-nothing government. Thus far in my life laziness has not been one of my sins. More than once people have remarked to me: 'Your capacity for work is not so small.' This year I have worked harder than ever before in my life. Therefore this charge of do-nothingism does not bother me very much."

So declared Prime Minister Abraham Kuyper from behind the ministerial Green Table in the parliamentary Second Chamber in The Hague on December 6, 1902.

Background

Kuyper was then 65, somewhat balding and quite plump in his premier's uniform. He had been in power for a year and a half and was relentlessly seeking to get his governmental programs off the ground. His public statement denying the charge of do-nothingism was a subtle affirmation that he was a life-long workaholic. Overwork as a student and later as Member of Parliament twice caused him to collapse and take extended periods of rest in 1860 and 1876-77. Kuyper learned, eventually, how to work intensively without overworking, and he had behind him a distinguished career of over 40 years as a pastor, publicist, theological professor, party leader and parliamentarian. Now he was a widower, for his wife, Johanna Kuyper-Schaay, had died in 1899 in Switzerland.

When Kuyper was in power, the population of the Netherlands was about five million. The East and West Indies colonial possessions were many times greater in territory and population than the Motherland. Governmental administration was a new task for Kuyper, especially since he was not a lawyer. Yet he did have significant experience in public affairs. His contacts with the Anti-Revolutionary elder statesman Groen van Prinsterer between 1864 and 1876 had strengthened his awareness of national and international affairs. He had organized and led the Anti-Revolutionary Party since 1872, a great organizational accomplishment in itself. He had served in Parliament during 1874-1875 and 1894-1901. He had taken various trips to England, Germany, France and Switzerland in the 1860s and 1870s. In 1898 he went to the United States of America (which he admired very much) to give his *Lectures on Calvinism* at Princeton Theological Seminary. But above all other accomplishments were the thousands of front-page editorials published in *The Standard* exploring every conceivable public matter from the Anti-Revolutionary viewpoint.

While Kuyper was Prime Minister of the Netherlands, the English Queen Victoria died in 1901 and was succeeded by King Edward VII and several Conservative cabinets governed England. Kaiser Wilhelm II was in charge of a powerful Germany, Franz Joseph I was Emperor of Austria-Hungary, Nicholas II was Tsar of Russia, and Theodore Roosevelt was President of the United States. Early in 1902 Queen Wilhelmina was seriously ill and the Kuyper Administration asked the Dutch people to pray for her recovery.

By late 1902 Kuyper was becoming accustomed to office and was enjoying it. He welcomed criticism of his policies from the confessional and secular parties. When

Opposition parliamentarians charged that he was a political manipulator, the Prime Minister took the charge good-naturedly. Awareness of the growing influence of the democratic Socialists and revolutionary Marxists can be seen in his public statements. The Kuyper Administration was not a "one issue government" because the Prime Minister saw the need to work for solutions to a whole range of problems including lower class poverty, educational injustice, public immorality and a just administration of the various governmental departments. During 1902 Kuyper made quite a few positive references to the Free Anti-Revolutionary leader, Jonkheer De Savornin Lohman; he appointed the Liberal leader P.W.A. Cort van der Linden to the advisory Council of State and exchanged polemics with the Socialist parliamentarian J.H. Schaper. But above all Kuyper's ministerial statements in 1902 reflected a politically spiritual witness rooted in his deep faith in Christ and the Scriptures.

Ministerial Statement

In early December the Prime Minister's office issued a written statement to Parliament designed to clarify the position of the Kuyper Cabinet and to correct certain misconceptions about its intentions. The secular leaders had expressed the fear that the Anti-Revolutionary-Catholic coalition government would eventually act in a theocratic way to repress the civil liberties of the secular parties and their members. The Kuyper statement emphasized that the ruling Christian parties and the cabinet did not act as a confessional government but as the national administration based on a majority parliamentary coalition. Thus the cabinet actively avoided the slightest appearance of theocratic repression. At the same time the cabinet policy of reforming the educational and Sunday laws was defended. Concerning the Sunday reform bill, it was emphasized that the only specifically Christian element was the day itself which those of diverse opinions supported.

The statement also affirmed that the state has a responsibility to work out the principle of neighborly love in public policy; this concept originated not with Christ but in the Old Testament (Leviticus 19:18). The Kuyper statement added that secular politicians had great difficulty seeing this integration of neighborly love with state policy even when it was before them. In the Netherlands, a rich Christian tradition had influenced governmental activities to a great extent: the Queen's recognizing that she reigns by the grace of God, the introducing of every bill in Parliament with a prayer as well as the prayer before the annual Speech from the Throne written by the Prime Minister and publicly read by the Queen. Furthermore, the various Dutch churches were free, and Christian morality was held in honor in marriage, paternal authority and concern for public decency.

On another topic the ministerial statement acknowledged that there were secondary disagreements within the governing coalition on such matters as military expenditures and the application of the death penalty. But such secondary disagreements were to be expected in a coalition. The charge that the cabinet was becoming more conservative and anti-democratic, a charge presumably made by a Socialist parliamentarian, was examined. To the anarchist, the democratic Socialist looked "conservative" and to the Socialist the Liberal looked "conservative." So the "conservative" charge was relative to the position of the politician doing the criticizing. The Minister of Internal Affairs (Kuyper) emphatically stated that his cabinet was not democratic in the Socialist sense of the term since the Marxist view defined "the people" as the lower class workers, yet the statement added that Kuyper was democratic in the sense of defining "the people" as inclusive of all classes. The Prime Minister was a Christian Democrat, and so he recognized, in distinction from the democratic Socialists, that human improvement involved both material and spiritual factors. His statement also flatly asserted that there could be no meaningful political cooperation between the Socialist party and the Christian Democratic parties since to cooperate would be a denial of the Christian confession.

The end of the Kuyper statement pointed out that several reform bills had been proposed during the previous year concerning the liberation of higher and secondary education, the modification of technical education, labor contracts and the regulations of pensions for teachers and their families. In addition, much time and effort had been devoted to the implementation of health and housing laws, the accident insurance act and the military criminal act. The normal administrative work in many departments had also been carried out as necessary.

From the Green Table

But Kuyper decided that a written statement was not enough. On December 6 the Prime Minister took his place behind the ministerial Green Table in the Second Chamber of the parliamentary Binnenhof. He intended to make clear the attitude and plans of the government and dispel misunderstandings.

Kuyper praised Lohman highly for his vocal support for a working majority on the parliamentary Right, speaking of him as a statesman who favored responsible support for the coalition cabinet. It is important to realize that Lohman had rejected Kuyper's progressive leadership in forming the Free Anti-Revolutionary Party several years earlier. While Lohman had refused a ministerial post in the cabinet, he had strongly supported the working majority supporting it. Kuyper's remarks make clear that he was deeply appreciative of this confidence in the cabinet. At the same time he was not afraid of criticism, for he remembered that Groen van Prinsterer had been criticized often for standing firm in his Anti-Revolutionary position. Since the Prime Minister felt he was holding Groen's position, he could not object to criticism. He would continue to defend his politically spiritual position inherited from the author of *Unbelief and Revolution*.

Then, in a very clear pronouncement, the Prime Minister outlined the goals of his Administration. "There are different groups in our country," he declared, "including a Christian segment of considerable size. This segment is still in an abnormal situation lacking the equal rights that other groups enjoy. Therefore the plan of this Cabinet is first of all to give a normal position to this segment, equal to the other groups. There is no thought of a privileged position for the Christian segment but merely equality with the others." Reappearing here is Kuyper's life-long goal of Christian emancipation. He seemed to be speaking of both Anti-Revolutionary and Catholic commoners denied access to the mainstream of national life. He affirmed that educational reforms on all levels were necessary to break the one-sided secular educational monopoly and to create space for those with a different world-view to take their places in society. The government's second goal, he asserted, was to retard and if possible, to end the demonic influences on society such as drunkenness, gambling, public indecency and pornography. Social legislation was planned to correct these public corruptions, legislation based on the Christian national traditions of marriage, family, church and authority in general. A third and final goal was to deal with rapid change caused by the industrial revolution. The government would introduce social legislation to protect the worker from dehumanizing forces. The Prime Minister ended his remarks by confessing that the omnipotent God is sovereign even over public law and over the Netherlands itself. All governing authority is derived from Him. Kuyper then returned to his office.

A few days later, on December 9, Kuyper again took his place behind the Green Table, this time to inform the Second Chamber of his two-stage plan to solve the education problem and to criticize the Marxist approach to social reform. The solution to the primary education problem, the Prime Minister said, would in the first stage be the passage of a bill designed to give private schools some immediate relief from pressure. In the second stage, a constitutional revision would be necessary to realize full educational equality between secular and Christian schools. Only the first stage, Kuyper declared, would be initiated by his cabinet.

The Socialist Schaper had raised a number of questions concerning democratic reformism and the plight of working people hoping to cause dissension within the confessional parties, between progressive and *status quo* elements. While Kuyper acknowledged that there were various types of workers' groups, he pointed out that the Socialists were seeking to entice members of the Protestant labor union, Patrimonium, and the Catholic People's Union to join the Socialist labor unions. Then he turned his attention to the difference between Socialist and Christian views of social reform. He said that he admired the coherence of the Marxist political and economic perspective; he admired such clarity of intention even while he rejected the system of thought. A Christian party, the Prime Minister went on, must seek to clarify the antithetical nature of the two opposing social systems. He wondered, "For whom will you choose: Marx or Christ?" Both are absolute alternatives. Marxism is based upon philosophical materialism, employs the tactics of the class struggle and reduces social life to material concerns. Likewise Christ forms the basis of a radically different world-view and a normative basis for action universally applicable. In response to Schaper's remark that there are two sets of texts in the Scriptures to which both the rich (for example, I Peter 2:13-19) and the poor (for example James 5:1-6) can appeal, Kuyper remarked: Whoever sets one set of texts against the other fails to appreciate the fullness of the person of Christ. The texts belong together because they speak both to the stewardship of owning property and to the need for social justice. The Christian segment of society must be strengthened through the Christian labor unions and parties to preserve an alternative to the steady growth of materialist influence. At the end of his speech, the Prime Minister, with a sense of urgency, made a promise: "We are continuing to appeal to the Christian parties to join forces even more closely. We will protest against everything within the Christian parties that denies the spirit of reform. We will also endeavor to promote in these parties a love and a desire for social reforms."

Conclusions

1. During the first year-and-a-half of Kuyper's government, he was struggling to initiate his policies. It takes any new head of government some time to get his programs off the ground. Since, by his own admission, Kuyper was new at national executive administration, during 1901-1902 he was learning what power was and how to use it.

2. Kuyper showed courage when he declared that his government was concerned with Christian emancipation and would work to put Christian commoners on an equal legal footing with all other groups in the society. He openly acknowledged the Christian basis of cabinet policy which was supported by a majority coalition of the confessional parties. He forcefully rejected the notion of a double standard of morality for individuals and states. He appealed to the Western Christian tradition as a partial support for his policies whenever possible. Before the Members of Parliament of all persuasions he unflinchingly stated the religious antithesis between Christianity and Marxism. Because of his concept of the antithesis and the relative weakness of the Socialists at that time, Kuyper refused to have any Socialists in his cabinet. But above all, as Prime Minister, Kuyper constantly affirmed that he was a Christian Democrat who would have nothing to do with theocratic repression.

3. Kuyper in power was concerned with the full range of governmental tasks. At the same time he felt that

certain matters were in urgent need of attention. In an unusually frank statement as Prime Minister, he encouraged a general criticism of his policies to promote better discussions in Parliament and better administrative policies. He let it be known that his official responsibility was to work for the realization of public justice for the whole people and not just for the higher or lower classes alone.

The Prime Minister in formal attire (Documentatiecentrum, Vrije Universiteit te Amsterdam courtesy of its director, Dr. George Puchinger).

Chapter 10

The Great Railroad Strike of 1903

"*C* HRISTIANITY IS PRESENTLY THE RELIGION *par excellence*, because it exhibits and manifests, to the fullest extent, the very nature and essence of every religious system, which is *the impoverishment, enslavement and annihilation of humanity for the benefit of divinity* . . . The idealistic abstraction, God, is a corrosive poison, which destroys and decomposes life, falsifies and kills it . . . In a word, we reject all legislation, all authority, and all privileged, licensed, official and legal influence, even though arising from universal suffrage, convinced that it can turn only to the advantage of a dominant minority of exploiters against the interests of the immense majority in subjection to them. This is the sense in which we are really Anarchists . . . The government of science and of men of science . . . or, again, disciples of the doctrinaire school of German Communism, cannot fail to be impotent, ridiculous, inhuman, cruel, oppressive, exploiting, maleficent."

These strong words were penned by the flamboyant Russian anarchist Michael Bakunin (1814-1876) and published in his famous declaration *God and the State*. Bakunin's career a century ago was similar to that of Che Guevara in the 1950s and 1960s: the tireless radical activist in search of new frontiers of revolutionary struggle. Bakunin sought to bring revolution to Germany, France and even to his native Russia just as Guevara, a close comrade of Fidel Castro, fought to bring communism to Cuba and Bolivia. *God and State*, first published in 1883 in French, was soon translated into German, Italian, Russian, Polish, Czech, Spanish, Rumanian, English, Yiddish and Dutch. The anarchistic message of Bakunin began to influence the European socialist movement.

But even as early as 1872 Karl Marx and Frederick Engels had to oust the anarchists personally from the International Workingmen's Association at its congress held in The Hague. Bakunin refused to submit to the dictatorial leadership of Marx. In 1891 the German Social Democratic Party issued its famous Erfurt Program which made maximum demands for the abolition of private property and minimum demands for realistic reforms. This Erfurt Program greatly influenced the European socialist movement. In the Netherlands the Social Democratic League, which included most of the followers of Domela Nieuwenhuis, decided at its 1893 Groningen congress to embark on a program of anti-parliamentary agitation. Those Socialists who favored parliamentary reform left the League to establish the Social Democratic Worker's Party led by the Frisian lawyer, P.J. Troelstra. For the next 25 years Troelstra was the leader of the Social Democratic Worker's Party while he also served as a member of the Dutch Parliament. Troelstra's party followed the Erfurt Program in its Marxist orientation; it worked for the socialization of the economy; it affirmed the validity of the class struggle and the necessity for an independent worker's party and allied trade unions; it called for universal suffrage for men and women, the abolition of the standing army, the nationalization of industry and transportation, an eight-hour work day, full insurance programs for workers to guard against accidents, sickness, old age and unemployment. In addition, Troelstra's Social Democrats expressed solidarity with the international labor movement and were hostile to the Dutch monarchy. But the more radical followers of the anarchist Bakunin also continued to be active within the Dutch labor movement.

Kuyper's coming to power was met with displeasure by the parliamentary Socialists of various hues who joined the minority Opposition. The anarchists on the outside were obviously upset both with Prime Minister Kuyper who affirmed the Christian Democratic basis of his government and with the Socialists who were willing to engage in traditional politics.

The Strike

During late December, 1902, the Prime Minister, who was also Minister of Internal Affairs, met with a large group of 141 workers as well as with an individual worker who told him that there was labor unrest among the dock workers in Amsterdam which might explode as a strike. Kuyper replied that he was aware of this labor unrest. But he was remaining neutral in order to consider the grievances of both labor and management. On January 11, 1903, a special meeting was held in Amsterdam of the Netherlandic Society of Railroad and Tram Personnel, a Social Democratic labor union. The union leader, J. Oudegeest, declared, "Our union will become strong enough to abolish the wage system only with the help of the progaganda of action." Oudegeest told the Socialist union members that a strike was an important part of labor politics.

On Thursday, January 29, the Amsterdam dock workers went on strike. Almost immediately the Netherlandic Society of Railroad and Tram Personnel under Oudegeest decided not to break the dock workers' strike. Thus the railroad workers at the main depot in Amsterdam as well as at Central Station went on strike. By Friday, January 30, the management of the Holland Railroad Company in Amsterdam had sent several

telegrams to the government in The Hague. The railroad
company seemed powerless in this situation. On Saturday, January 31, the local Amsterdam strike widened to
become a national railroad strike affecting such important urban centers as Rotterdam, Haarlem, Amersfoort
and The Hague. While maintaining a neutral stance between labor and management, Prime Minister Kuyper
had essential mail transported by automobile, mobilized
the national militia, consulted with the Royal Engineers
as to what could be done technically and ordered 860 army troops to be rushed to Amsterdam. Only 500 troops
were kept in The Hague to protect the government. A
news flash reported that at Durgerdam, northeast of the
Amsterdam city limits, strike-breakers were beaten up by
militant strikers. By Saturday evening the management of
the Holland Railroad Company admitted that it was
powerless against the strikers.

On Sunday, February 1, Troelstra's paper *The People* expressed solidarity with the striking transport
workers, calling the strike the heart of the worker's movement. The Socialist paper urged the formation of an even
more militant unity to force the government to grant
universal suffrage. But the strike was itself being led by
Oudegeest and a small group of 150 militants. During the
day the municipal workers of Amsterdam threatened to
poison the city's water supply. A carriage driver's strike
also took place in the city, preventing physicians from
visiting their patients. By Sunday evening the national
railroad strike was over, but a general spirit of anarchy
was in the air. A second strong statement supporting the
use of strike tactics to further the proletarian cause
against the state, the police and captains of industry was
published in *The People* on Tuesday, February 3. On
Wednesday the Kuyper government issued a brief statement expressing its sympathy for the plight of the
Holland Railroad Company, unable to carry out its
responsibilities due to the strike. The serious implications
of this strike would continue to occupy the government

and the Parliament during February, March and April and to a lesser extent throughout 1903.

Anti-Strike Bills

Prime Minister Kuyper appeared in Parliament on February 25. His remarks were brief but very important. Kuyper admitted that the government had been unprepared for the January strike and thus had not had the means to deal with it adequately. He also pointed to loopholes in the law that had to be covered to deal with such national strikes. The Prime Minister announced that three bills were being introduced in Parliament. The first called for the creation of a national railroad brigade which would prevent, by force if necessary, such railroad strikes occurring in the future. The second bill provided for the creation of a State Commission to investigate the grievances of railroad personnel. Kuyper's third bill called for an investigation of possible criminal acts committed by the strikers; it was intended to prevent workers from being coerced into wrong-doing in the future. The Prime Minister then appealed to all the parliamentary parties who were concerned with upholding the rule of law to support these bills. Kuyper emphasized that the government was not engaging in reactionary vengeance but that social reform was the goal. It is in the interest of all the parties, the Prime Minister concluded, that legal authority be maintained. The head of government then returned to his office.

Due to the national concern about security against terrorism, the Prime Minister made long statements behind the Green Table on March 10 and 11. He reported to Parliament on the events of the national crisis, emphasizing that the government had made a cautious response to the crisis, having had only a small armed force at its disposal and wanting to prevent a disaster such as had recently happened during massive American strikes in Pittsburgh and Chicago. The government also wanted to avoid acting rashly. The task of the government, the Prime Minister emphasized, was not only to restore order but to maintain order in an atmosphere of calmness. The creation of such an atmosphere was essential, given the spirit of anarchism then visible. The Prime Minister then affirmed that he would not reveal in advance what he would do in a future massive strike. He acknowledged the unusual character of the great railroad strike and that its main purpose was to agitate for universal suffrage. The task of the government, Kuyper continued, was to protect the rights of all social groups while upholding the authority delegated to it alone, the authority essential for national tranquility and order. The government would never abdicate its unique task but would defend its authority with force if necessary, according to the Prime Minister. But he reiterated that the government take seriously the legitimate grievances of the workers by means of the state investigation committee. Troelstra accused the government of using force to stop the great strike, and Kuyper responded by declaring that while the Prime Minister firmly believed in the legitimacy of labor unions, Troelstra had, in fact, exploited unionism to further Socialist goals. Kuyper recognized the right to strike but not to break contracts. There had just been a sharp debate on the question of unionism between the Socialist Troelstra, and the Minister of Waterworks, Trade and Industry, J.C. de Marez Oyens, who had carried out governmental orders during the great strike. Thus there was great tension in the Chamber. Kuyper added that workers' strikes and lock-outs by employers were both weapons that could lead to terrorism. The Prime Minister told the Chamber that the choice was between constitutional government and the use of clandestine terrorism.

The three anti-strike bills were then debated, receiving the support of all the parties except the Socialist groups. A Defense Committee was established by the Socialist trade unions, the Social Democratic Worker's Party and the Free Socialists to oppose these laws. The

Prime Minister took part in the debate on the anti-strike bills on April 4. He warmly thanked the parties of the Right for their positive verbal support for these bills, and also expressed appreciation to the Liberals in the Left Opposition for their support. He emphasized that these bills had to be passed in order to clarify the legal position and the security of railroad personnel. The events of late January and early February had laid upon the Prime Minister the heavy burden of deciding on the proper long-term action the government should take. He was determined to eliminate the terrorism of a small group which acted as a secret government. The anarchists and their Social Democratic friends, Kuyper continued, had a different set of norms on law, contract-breaking, and striking than those embraced within the national constitutional heritage. He quoted Dr. W.H. Nolens, a Catholic legislator, as saying that the anarchists and Social Democrats were outside the nationally accepted social-ethical consensus because of their materialistic world-view. The Prime Minister stated flatly that the railroad strike was a criminal offense because it upset essential transportation services with grave economic, military, political and diplomatic consequences. The integrity and effectiveness of the state had been defied. He ended his remarks by an appeal for the anti-strike bills to be passed.

It was then that the Defense Committee called for a general strike to protest the bills and defy the Kuyper Administration. But the anti-strike bills were passed into law, and the general strike failed miserably. The anarchists accused the legislator Troelstra and the union leader Oudegeest of betrayal. Troelstra's Social Democratic Worker's Party was discredited in the eyes of the general public.

Conflict and Conviction

From the Green Table the Prime Minister defended his anti-strike policy in the face of criticism during the fall of 1903. Troelstra had charged the government of acting in a criminal way on this matter. Kuyper responded on September 22 by pointing out that there were two views of criminality in operation, each based upon a different view of normativity. The Social Democrats, he thundered, had put themselves outside the national ethical consensus by their moral relativism. The term "criminal turbulence" used in the Speech from the Throne just delivered by Queen Wilhelmina was a proper description of the revolutionary plot which had resulted in the national railroad strike. Kuyper then asserted that this strike, from the viewpoint of the Christian Democratic parties, had been ultimately an attack on God's authority for the constitutional state.

In early December the Prime Minister's office issued a statement which admitted that the turbulence between January and April had occupied so much public attention that the backlog of bills on labor, social insurance, sickness and old-age insurance, and liquor problems had not been considered properly. The statement regretted such inaction on these important social questions and expressed the hope that these bills would be presented when ready. The ministerial statement also disputed the humanist assertion of a basic difference between anarchists and democratic Socialists. In a crisis, the statement continued, they would stand together in support of the class struggle. The statement rejected both Karl Marx and Michael Bakunin, presumably for their common commitment to revolution.

The Prime Minister appeared behind the Green Table on December 4 to make a response to Troelstra's charge that Anti-Revolutionaries were two-faced in their use of Christian ethics. In Troelstra's view, Christian ethics included both an appeal to authority and a condemnation of the love of Mammon. The Socialist leader charged that during the strike the Anti-Revolutionaries had been concerned only to maintain authority with no thought of the exploitation of the poor. The Prime

Minister began by declaring that Christian ethics are based on the commandments to love God and neighbor. On this foundation, Catholics and Anti-Revolutionaries believed that governmental authority has divine origin. Likewise, Kuyper continued, the command of neighborly love required help for the oppressed which the cabinet recognized by its social reform program. Authority had been maintained, the Prime Minister went on, and the official investigation was begun to examine the grievances of the railroad workers. He contrasted Troelstra's humanistic view of state authority, based upon popular sovereignty, with the Reformed belief in divine authority as the basis of the state. Kuyper expressed his conviction that the state must seek to honor God since it is tied to the divine will. Concerning the "Socialist Jesus" used by proletarians to win Christian workers to the red banner, the Prime Minister pointed out that such portrayals emphasized Jesus' denunciation of the injustices of rich against poor while purposely ignoring the saving work of the incarnate Christ. At the same time Kuyper admitted the partial positive value of the Socialist critique of social ills. He also responded to Troelstra's charge that in Kuyper's "Maranatha" speech of 1891, reference was made only to ethical persuasion and not to force. The Prime Minister said that his original reference had been against an illegitimate policy of theocratic oppression; however, revolutionary defiance was another matter which required the legitimate use of force as a last resort to restore order. The Prime Minister noted that both Calvinists and Socialists were driven by strong concepts of purpose. However, the Socialists were concerned only with worldly success. The strength of the Christian Democrats, by contrast, was found in their hope of heaven as the reward for their labors.

Then with great politically spiritual insight, Prime Minister Kuyper brought into focus the basic issue raised by the public debate on the great railroad strike:

Mr. Chairman, after listening to the twenty-five speakers who preceded me, I want to make a few concluding remarks. The recent discussion in this Chamber concerns the nature of law. But a basic difficulty arises when God is eliminated from law since legal certainty also vanishes. I know that many people have tried to find this certainty in the written law. But human codified law is in itself an insufficient basis for law. There must be a higher authority than written law; this is the question that is presently being debated. From the viewpoint of the Koran and the Jews, there is an absolute revelation of law which cannot be applied in new ways. On the other hand, under Christian leadership, law must be sought which is not inflexible, but which can be applied according to differences in time, place and circumstance. In response to Troelstra and Marx, we Christians say that the standard for law is not found in men, but that the idea of law comes from God. But because man is created in God's image, he too, has an idea of the highest law that is universally valid as determined by God's control over the world. It has been asked why we also oppose the Liberals when the Socialists have caused the present danger. My response is that neither Anti-Revolutionaries nor Catholics will limit their struggle to merely opposing Social Democrats because in doing so they would lose their own distinctive principles. The great antithesis between Liberals and what they term "clericals" is that the Liberals ignore God's revelation. We derive revelation not only from the Holy Scriptures but also from nature and reason while recognizing that the defects of nature and reason must have the necessary corrective of Special Revelation.

The Prime Minister then left the Green Table to return to his office. The great railroad strike of 1903 was history.

Afterthoughts

1. The great railroad strike of 1903 was a major contest between the Kuyper government and the Socialists of that time. Kuyper's leadership was put to a severe test in this early example of a confrontation often seen today between Christian Democrats and Socialists/Marxists/Anarchists in several European countries.

2. In the views of the Dutch public, Prime Minister

Kuyper was the winner in the contest with the strikers. This was partially due to his cautious military response, the passage of anti-strike laws, and his concern to examine the legitimate grievances of the strikers. Yet some Liberal critics accused Kuyper of using the strike as an excuse for not pushing his social reform legislation with sufficient vigor.

3. The great railroad strike gave Kuyper the opportunity to point out that political conflict is not merely political, but is ultimately a matter of clashing religious world-views. Kuyper's magnificent articulation of a Christian basis for public law and state authority in contrast to the humanistic relativism of the Liberals and Socialists was an important contribution to the debate. We need such politically spiritual insight into public affairs today.

The Prime Minister emphasized that the government serves the national interest, not the concerns of one party (Documentatiecentrum, Vrije Universiteit te Amsterdam courtesy of its director, Dr. George Puchinger).

Chapter 11

The Higher Education Debate in 1904

"**T**HE STATE UNIVERSITIES ARE NOT at issue since they are in no way affected by this higher education bill. The income, honor, influence and autonomous character of the state universities are left entirely intact. What is requested in this bill is that other groups in the country desiring alternatives on the basis of sacred conviction be given the opportunity to develop. The representative from Zutphen says that if this small right were granted to the academic group desiring to defend Christian conviction in scholarship, it would be a disaster for the country and pernicious for the people. Mr. Speaker, I accept this statement as it was delivered because I view the distinguished representative from Zutphen not only as the standard-bearer but also as the spokesman of the parliamentary Left. The Left considers it a disaster for the country and pernicious for the people if the Christian life-view be better able to be maintained in scholarship than has been the case up to the present."

These important words on the need for the complete liberation of Christian higher education were uttered by Prime Minister Abraham Kuyper before a packed Second Chamber at the height of the higher education debate on February 25, 1904. The lines were drawn clearly between the secular intolerance of the parliamentary Left and the appeal for educational pluralism by members of the Right. The debate on the higher education bill was carried on at a high level. Such important political spokesmen as Theodorus Heemskerk (Anti-Revolutionary), Professor P.J.M. Aalberse (Catholic), Jonkheer A.F. de Savornin Lohman (Christian Historical) and Mgr. W.H. Nolens (Catholic) made vigorous defenses of the bill. Those who attacked the bill included Professor W. Van der Vlugt (Liberal), P.J. Troelstra (Social Democratic) and the entire Left. Surprisingly Dr. J. Th. de Visser (Christian Historical) also opposed this bill. But the man who led the debate was Kuyper himself.

Kuyper as Educator

Kuyper was no stranger to academic questions. He had received the Th.D. from the University of Leiden in 1862 having written a Latin thesis on an important aspect of the origins of the Dutch Reformed Church during the Reformation. He was professor of theology at the Free University of Amsterdam from 1880 to 1901. During most of that time he exercised academic leadership as Rector of the Free University. During the early 1890s he lectured on the five faculties comprising a university (theology, natural science, medicine, letters and law). His three-volume *Encyclopedia of Sacred Theology* was an important study on the structure and content of theological thought. Kuyper also had lectured on such important topics as common grace and the task of the state in a secular society. A general theory of pluralism that had emerged in his thought since 1869 was vitally important to his program for the liberation of university-level education.

Kuyper's Bill

The Prime Minister acting as Minister of Internal Affairs, submitted his higher education bill to Parliament on March 11, 1903. The bill was designed to complete the legal status of non-public higher education, technical higher education and non-public preparatory higher education. The main provision of the bill was that non-public higher educational institutions would receive the right to grant degrees *(effectus civilis)* for governmental professions equal in value to those awarded at the state universities. Such private institutions would also be given some financial subsidies from public funds. The bill also provided for the creation of a technical university. Finally, the bill made legal provision for the establishment of special chairs representing non-public academic associations at the state universities. It is important to remember that at the time, the Free University of Amsterdam was the only such non-public academic institution. Later, however, the Catholics received equal benefits when they established the Catholic University at Nijmegen in 1923, as did a number of other groups of various persuasions when they established academic institutions.

The most important parliamentary debates on this higher education bill took place during February and March of 1904. Kuyper's contribution to this debate included some of his best speeches in the Second Chamber. A Liberal journalist, C.K. Elout, who was present in the parliamentary gallery during these debates, was impressed at the high level of discussion on this academic matter. It was a fundamental debate on the right, pro and con, for non-public universities to grant academic degrees of full value. Of all the speakers, journalist Elout commented, Kuyper was by far the best speech-maker. The small but sturdy Prime Minister expressed his views dynamically from behind the Green Table to a full House of attentive listeners. Drawing up his shoulders as if ready for battle, Kuyper made careful use of a strong voice that could be easily heard throughout the Chamber. Rhetorical gestures and humor were used sparingly but with great effect. According to this Liberal eyewitness Kuyper could conjure up a rhetorical majority for his argument by his skillful use of oratorical talents. Many in the country and even some in the Parliament came under the spell of his rhetoric.

The February 24 Speech

The Prime Minister began to make his case for the bill on February 24, 1904. He thanked Heemskerk, Lohman and Mgr. Nolens for their public defense of the bill. Prof. Van der Vlugt had previously told the Chamber that of the sixteen appointments the Prime Minister made to state university professorships only two were believers. Kuyper explained that approving these royal professorial nominations which originated in the Universities themselves, meant that he did not seek to disrupt the established system of academic appointments which operated between the Crown, the state universities and the government. There was no thought of using theocratic pressure, since Holland was constitutionally a non-Christian state. At the same time the Prime Minister advocated the creation of private chairs at public universities as provided for in his bill.

The leader's attention then turned to the motivating spirit of the bill: the complete liberation of higher education. During the seventeenth century the Netherlandic state had been officially confessional while lacking true pluralistic and academic freedoms. It was only with the Constitution of 1848 that such educational freedom was permitted in principle. The word "free" as defined by the Prime Minister meant "free from government control" or "non-public." The term "liberation" carried the same pluralistic connotation. From this viewpoint, the creation of many free universities within a pluralistic academic setting was to be encouraged.

The Higher Education Law of 1876, the Prime Minister emphasized, defined this freedom more carefully in its provisions that properly prepared students could take the state examinations in their academic areas even if they had not studied at the public universities. The

1876 law also permitted private foundations and churches to establish institutions of higher learning and to receive partial public funding. The problem with this law was that students at a private university were required to take two sets of examinations in order to get a *bona fide* degree. In effect, this required students to follow an academic program at both a private and a public university.

In the Prime Minister's view such a requirement was demoralizing for these students. He reflected on the great nervousness and exhaustion he experienced when taking exams at the University of Leiden between 1855 and 1862. Thus the bill sought to grant to private universities the right to award academic degrees which would be equal to those of the public universities and which would meet the standards for possible governmental service. Students from non-public institutions would be required to give a public defense of their doctoral dissertations to demonstrate their learning competence to all. Kuyper pointed out the important contributions made by non-public institutions such as the Catholic University of Louvain, Belgium, the Free University of Brussels, Belgium, the Johns Hopkins University, Baltimore, Maryland, Harvard University in Cambridge, Massachusetts and the University of Pennsylvania in Philadelphia. He strongly refuted the charge that the Free University of Amsterdam was nothing more than a school of indoctrination with a narrow-minded faculty ignorant of true scholarship. The published dissertations and orations from this institution were cited as evidence of on-going serious academic reflection. Kuyper made reference to the comment of the skeptical theologian Allard Pierson at the opening of the Free University in 1880 to the effect that this private institution would help the lower classes to improve themselves by educating their promising sons. Logically, then, equalization of the value of non-public degrees with public diplomas would speed up this emancipation process. After the Prime Minister finished, the Chamber gradually emptied.

The February 25 Speech

When the Prime Minister took his place behind the Green Table on the following day, his remarks related to the bill under discussion, concerning the purpose of the university and the nature of scholarship. Kuyper began by emphasizing that this bill was designed to do justice to all types of non-public universities including those established by Catholics, Calvinists and secularists.

Kuyper defined a university as an institution designed to educate students and to be involved in academic scholarship. With thanks to Prof. Van der Vlugt the Prime Minister declared that academic scholarship involved the accumulation of knowledge, the ability to discern truth from error and the use of scholarly research methods. A university should be composed of the five main faculties. Kuyper, as a former academician, lamented the fact that professors usually neglect informal discussions with students. Kuyper felt such contacts helped improve the educational process.

With the basic religious antithesis in mind, Kuyper outlined the two major approaches to learning which he termed the indifferent and the principled systems. The indifferent system was a supermarket of life options and academic viewpoints such as could be found at the state universities. Such an invitation to subjectivism often resulted in students embracing skepticism. Van der Vlugt was singled out as a champion of this "indifferent system." In contrast to such indifference to truth, the Prime Minister advocated the principled system based on a fundamental presupposition for academic research. From this viewpoint the slogan is "only the truth." An academic institution in this system would be based on a common foundational conviction with room for minor disagreements. Thus the Catholic University of Louvain encouraged scholarly discussion and disagreement within a Roman Catholic framework, not allowing its professors to become Lutheran or Reformed.

The Prime Minister then outlined his view of Christian scholarship within the principled system. Scholarship is systematic learning of a universal and academic nature. Christian scholarship confesses a belief in the Creator God of Scripture and in the organic unity of the cosmos. God is the original Thinker, Kuyper added, and man is to think His thoughts after Him in an academic fashion. Kuyper affirmed the importance of the cultural mandate given to mankind at the beginning of history for systematic learning. Likewise, the recognition of the organic unity between body and soul is important for one's world-view. Christian scholarship would acknowledge the essential character of faith, the presence of sin in the world, and the scriptural revelation of the salvation found in Christ. Due to the basic antithesis between belief and unbelief, there could be no common ground between the basic principles of Christian and non-Christian learning. Kuyper rejected the attempts of the secularists to label their brand of scholarship as "orthodox" and that of their opponents as "sectarian." The government was not competent to decide what true scholarship is, the Prime Minister maintained. "There can only be talk of fairness and justice," Kuyper thundered, "when every principled viewpoint is represented not merely in one academic discipline but in all of them with complete equality!"

Near the end of his speech the Prime Minister pointed out that there were two distinct groups in the country, those who favored continued Liberal intolerance in university education and those who advocated true academic pluralism. It was the latter group, desiring educational alternatives on the basis of sincere conviction, that he wanted to help with this bill. With his remarks completed, the Prime Minister left the Chamber.

Additional Comments

Between March 3 and 15 the Prime Minister spent a great deal of time responding to specific objections to his bill in Parliament. During this period his statements included autobiographical comments and concluding remarks.

The autobiographical comments shed some light on the deeper motivations which moved Kuyper to argue for complete academic pluralism along institutional lines. He recalled his own spiritual difficulties as a theological student at the University of Leiden in the late 1850s in which his piety was replaced by a corrosive theological rationalism. His professor, the famous modernist J.H. Scholten, advocated the new life-view while clinging to a belief in miracles simply because his modernist position had not reached a consistent conclusion. Kuyper experienced the fires of doubt in an atmosphere of the moral shamelessness of student life. Many were the hours, he admitted, during which his father, Rev. J.F. Kuyper, patiently talked with him, trying to free young Abraham from rationalism and restore him to faith. But Rev. Kuyper even though he was a university man, failed because he could not adequately refute the latest philosophical and scholarly arguments of his son the theological student. It was only after leaving the university, the Prime Minister confessed, that he was restored to faith in Christianity. Kuyper also noted that the intelligentsia had broken with orthodoxy to embrace various forms of cultured unbelief in thought and life. Thus Kuyper put a high priority on the integration of Christian faith and learning.

At another point in the discussion, Kuyper noted that when the previous higher education bill was debated in the Chamber during 1876-77 he had been a Member of Parliament for Gouda but had been unable to participate in the proceedings because he had been out of the country recovering from physical exhaustion. Since he was present and in power in 1904, he was anxious to make the best possible case for his higher education bill. Kuyper declared that his own conviction that faith in Christ is the basis of absolute truth was the common conviction of the parliamentary Right. He made such statements about truth and unbelief after a generation of reflection in theological circles.

Kuyper's concluding remarks were his final defense of the bill. He denied that this legislative proposal was designed to promote the Free University, arguing that it would meet a universal need for academic pluralism. He emphasized the neutrality of the cabinet towards any social group in its advocacy of this bill. The promotion of the liberation of university education was the desired goal, not favoritism towards a particular group. Such a liberation, Kuyper felt, was necessary since the evolutionary world-view dominated the state universities. He asserted that secularist educators were the intolerant representatives of a modern clericalism that opposed pluralism. Given the secular anarchy of ideas in the public institutions, Kuyper saw these universities as ultimately being based on strong personalities. He wanted, alongside them, non-public institutions based upon principles. He even went so far as to declare that the public universities would actually be improved by the introduction of special professorial chairs supported by non-public institutions. Allowing such institutions to grant bona fide degrees was much more important to the bill than the awarding of subsidies. Kuyper's affirmation of the basic antithesis between Christian and non-Christian views was firmly based on the fundamental truths embraced by all those in the tradition of religious orthodoxy. The antithesis was between revealed Christianity and secularistic naturalism.

On March 11, 1904 the Prime Minister made the following clear statement on the matter near the end of the debate:

> . . . the modern world-view and its idea of scholarship as defended by the parliamentary Left affirms that *scholarship is the judge over divinely-given Revelation*. This brings us to the general question. Strongly affirmed in varying degrees by the parliamentary Right is the opposite position: from Revela-

tion, a Christian world-view is derived, antithetical in character to the new world-view. We are firmly convinced that this antithesis is permanent and extends to every branch of scholarship. Therefore I saw that finally history will pass judgment on this matter. The only means to bring the struggle between the world-views to a desired solution is by the unhindered development of both perspectives which are precious to us of the Left and Right. But such a solution is rejected by the Opposition. The Left wants Christian scholarship to be kept in bondage while its own brand of scholarship keeps the exclusive privilege it presently enjoys and will later extend to insure its final triumph.

On March 24 the higher education bill was passed by the Second Chamber but then it was rejected by the Opposition-controlled First Chamber. Sensing that the First Chamber was out of step with popular opinion, the Prime Minister asked Queen Wilhelmina to dissolve that body and call for new elections, which she did on July 19. After the First Chamber elections, Kuyper reintroduced his higher education bill on March 9, 1905. The First Chamber passed it on May 20, and the Queen signed it into law two days later. The Higher Education Law of 1905 became a fact of history and a source of educational justice in the liberation of Christian scholarship.

Reflections

1. The granting of the right for non-public universities to award bona fide degrees (the right of *effectus civilis*) was a turning point in Kuyper's life. One of the most important goals of his career was achieved: the liberation of higher education. He did not use his power to crush the public universities but to create legal space for non-public institutions to compete with them on an equal footing in a pluralist system. This pluralism was impartial; it was designed to make viable all such non-public universities of Calvinist, Catholic and other persuasions. At the same time the Higher Education law of 1905 was an immediate help to the Free University of Amsterdam and later to the Catholic University of Nijmegen, founded in 1923.

2. One of Kuyper's personal motivations for fighting for this Higher Education Law of 1905 was to give Christian students an alternative to the difficulties he experienced with academic unbelief during his university days forty years earlier. In order to get this bill passed into law Kuyper resorted to the unusual but constitutional means of having the Queen dissolve the First Chamber in order to get a Christian Democratic majority elected in that body. The Opposition strongly questioned this tactic.

3. These speeches were a powerful witness to Kuyper's faith that the Gospel of Christ is relevant for both salvation and scholarship based upon revealed truth normative for all of life. Kuyper criticized the non-Christian character of scholarship achieved by men who believed themselves autonomous. For perhaps the first time Kuyper began to use the term "antithesis" to describe the basic clash between the Christian and humanist world-views. Clearly, Kuyper rejected the notion of neutral common ground between scholarly belief and unbelief.

The elder statesman as grandfather (Documentatiecentrum, Vrije Universiteit te Amsterdam courtesy of its director, Dr. George Puchinger).

Chapter 12

The Struggle Against Intemperance

A T THE TURN OF THE CENTURY in America and Europe, the growth of secular life-styles among both rich and poor had spawned the search for pleasure in bars, taverns, beer halls, pubs, theatres, cabarets, night clubs and exclusive country clubs. The pursuit of wine, women and song became a great passion for many. Every major urban center like New York, London, Paris and Amsterdam had its night life. Along with this night life went gambling, fights, stealing, drunkenness, frivolity and even prostitution. Alcoholism and immorality were the natural results of night life and pleasure-seeking. The rich got drunk to celebrate their wealth, while the poor drank too much gin to forget their misery. But people of both classes adopted an attitude of living for the pleasures of the moment at the expense of the future. Thus the problems of night life and drunkenness were related to the larger social questions of poverty, poor housing, infidelity, broken homes, labor exploitation, social dislocation, secular values and the quest for the life of luxury.

Personal Experience

The immediate cause for Prime Minister Abraham Kuyper to express his views on this subject was the expiration of the liquor law on May 1, 1904. Between April 26 and June 10, 1904, Kuyper spent a great deal of time and

effort attempting to convince parliamentarians to adopt a
proper revision of this liquor legislation. The general aim
of the Kuyper Administration on this subject, as stated in
the Speech from the Throne in 1901, was to curb the
misuse of intoxicating beverages.

At this point mention of Kuyper's own experience
might explain his public statements concerning the revision of the expired liquor legislation. At the University of
Leiden, young Abraham had been a member of a student drinking club in the early 1860s. But with his conversion in the mid-1860s, Kuyper stopped attending such
clubs. As a pastor he strongly felt a Christian should not
attend bars, taverns and similar places where alcoholic
beverages were served because of the lax morals
associated with such establishments. While serving as a
pastor at the (Reformed) New Church in Amsterdam
from 1870 to 1874, he became aware of the problems of
urban poverty, poor housing and alcoholism. He also
noticed the many cafés in the Kalverstraat and
Fredericksplein areas of Amsterdam where great numbers
of people socialized. When Kuyper was on his American
tour in 1898, he lunched in a large hotel on Fifth Avenue
in New York City. He was amazed that out of several hundred luncheon guests only a handful were having wine
with their meal. When Kuyper commented on this
phenomenon, a parliamentarian interjected that this
handful of drinkers must have been Dutchmen!

When Kuyper gave his famous *Lectures on
Calvinism* at Princeton Theological Seminary in
Princeton, New Jersey, also in 1898, he revealed his attitude toward secular entertainment in general. He felt it
was improper for Christians to make a habit of card playing, theatre-going, or popular dancing. Card playing involved gambling and an appeal to luck to win money.
The secular theatre was promoted by the questionable
moral atmosphere in which the actors and actresses lived.
Popular dancing, likewise, often involved a compromise
of moral purity. Kuyper emphasized that there was

nothing evil in the playing cards themselves. He highly valued the plays of Shakespeare and the ancient Greek dramas. He did not protest against the dance as an art form. But he did object to leisure pursuits that put in jeopardy biblical standards of conduct. Alcoholism contributed to this problem of conduct.

(From time to time Kuyper went on trips, sometimes to the Alps to do some mountain climbing or hiking. After a long trek he enjoyed relaxing with a glass of beer. While not a total abstainer, he was very moderate and made a distinction between beer and wine, on the one hand, and hard liquor on the other.)

Revised Bill

The immediate cause for the parliamentary debate on this question was the revision of the expired legislation on the retail sales of hard liquor. The Prime Minister began his remarks with some general observations about this social problem of drinking. There were three groups in society: (1) a large group of non-drinkers, (2) the many moderates who had a daily glass and/or who occasionally had something to drink at a celebration, and (3) a small group of alcoholics who had a negative influence on the community. Kuyper termed alcoholism a fatal social poison that had serious physical, psychological, motivational and ethical consequences. Studies were cited to show that drunkenness was related to physical and mental disorders, to criminality, chronic poverty, disease, illegitimacy and prostitution. A French expert who had studied this problem was quoted as declaring that alcoholism is a modern scourge. How could society be protected against the cancer of alcoholism? The Prime Minister felt that the answer was to be found in the spiritual conversion of people to Christ, a public opinion which favored high moral standards, the efforts of the churches and other Christian social organizations to help fight alcoholism, and legislation designed to create a legal climate unfavorable to the spread of unrestrained intemperance. Kuyper had high praise for the work of the Salvation Army with the urban poor afflicted with the evils of drunkenness. Recognition was made that this problem was first of all a problem of sin in the human heart that could only be transformed by the Gospel of Christ in a ministry of social compassion. The churches, Christian teachers and confessional labor unions all had vital roles to play in this field. The Prime Minister emphasized that while legislation was important, it could not by itself solve the problems of intemperance.

The governmental bill was designed to curb the misuse of hard liquor, especially the offenses of bootlegging and drunkenness. It was hoped that the numbers of speakeasies would be reduced. This bill was to protect those who could not protect themselves, those suffering from the corrupting influences of urban slums and the many bars in those areas. Following the English example, the bill called for a distinction between liquor licenses awarded to bars and those granted to package stores. Kuyper's reasoning, based upon the successful experience with package stores in England, was significant. Intoxicating beverages bought by the bottle in a package store were cheaper than those purchased by the glass in a bar. Most often bottled beverages would be taken home to be consumed. This would tend to discourage workmen, for example, from spending their nights in the questionable atmosphere of the bars. The Prime Minister believed that it was better for a man to have his daily glass of wine at home with his wife than at a tap room. Kuyper denounced the bar as the "drunkard's temple" and the "dark tunnel to social corruption." He argued that the creation of special licenses for package stores where alcoholic beverages would be sold by the bottle but were not to be consumed on the premises would tend to discourage moderates from becoming drunkards. The atmosphere of a package store would be like that of a grocery store. Kuyper emphasized that the bill was directed only against the misuse of strong drink. Those under the age of eighteen were not to be admitted to either pubs or package stores. Kuyper hoped that the bill would be an aid to moral improvement by curbing bad drinking customs.

In addition the Prime Minister gave several general suggestions as to how moral opposition to drunkenness could be furthered. The state could adopt a policy of hiring non-drinkers for public service positions while firing alcoholics. The government should also subsidize half-way houses to help alcoholics seeking to be cured of their problems. Kuyper also favored the creation of fruit juice clubs by private groups to provide sociability without liquor.

At the end of the parliamentary debate, the revised law on the retail sales of hard liquor became a reality along the lines outlined by Kuyper. Thus this episode in Prime Minister Kuyper's struggle against intemperance came to a satisfactory end.

Observations

1. Kuyper was dealing with a concrete legislative problem inherited from previous governments as well as with a serious social problem. As a responsible head of government, he had to face these problems as he found them.

2. He recognized that intemperance was ultimately a spiritual problem with serious physical, psychological, moral and social consequences beyond the ability of government to solve single-handedly. Conversion to Christ and the further ministries of various Christian groups were needed to change the motivation and outlook of alcoholics. Government could only seek to protect society from the corruptions of intemperance by passing and enforcing relevant legislation.

3. Kuyper realized that total prohibition would be counter-productive. He was familiar with American prohibitionism. His view was confirmed with the failure of prohibition (the repealed eighteenth amendment to the

Constitution) in the United States in the 1920s and 1930s.

4. The Prime Minister's strategy was to create an alliance between non-drinkers and moderates to curb alcoholism. It was hoped that the introduction of a special category of liquor licenses for package stores would encourage adults to have a glass of wine at home rather than at a bar. Kuyper preferred a man to have his glass of wine or gin at home with his wife rather than in the questionable atmosphere of the neighborhood tavern. Thus the home and the package store were seen as discouragements to the alcoholic night life.

5. In the revised bill the Prime Minister's attack was against the morally corrupting influence of the saloon. This was a typical attitude of most social reformers of the day.

6. In his personal life Kuyper occasionally enjoyed alcoholic beverages. However, great moderation was to be exercised in their use, and all morally questionable worldly amusements were to be avoided. Kuyper considered the patronage of bars to be improper conduct for believers. But he did approve of a glass at home for reasons of health and relaxation (important in a day of less medical care and no central heating in damp Holland). In his general approach to Christian liberty, amusements and the use of alcoholic beverages, Kuyper was reflecting a Puritan position which he had inherited from previous centuries.

Kuyper as Elder Statesman

1905-1918

Kuyper in Athens, Greece, in 1906 (Documentatiecentrum, Vrije Universiteit te Amsterdam courtesy of its director, Dr. George Puchinger).

Chapter 13

The Transition

P RIME MINISTER ABRAHAM KUYPER's years in power were stormy ones indeed. Much like some recent American presidents embroiled in controversy, he was either hated or loved. It was virtually impossible to be neutral toward Kuyper. As the parliamentary election of 1905 approached, partisan political tensions intensified. The Prime Minister's antithesis perspective and pluralist political record had aroused the hatred of the Liberal-Socialist Opposition and had also caused discord within the Anti-Revolutionary Party itself.

The results of this controversy were felt long after 1905 and marked Kuyper's painful transition to the status of elder statesman, never again to serve as the nation's chief executive though always wielding great influence over the Calvinist commoners.

Campaign of 1905

During the years of the Kuyper Administration, some important changes took place within several of the political parties. In 1904 the Catholics organized themselves in a national network of voter's clubs with the name of the Roman Catholic Political Party under the leadership of Dr. W.H. Nolens and P.J.M. Aalberse. In January, 1905, the Liberal Union and Liberal Democratic parties signed a common election platform calling for a constitutional revision, the ratification of an article to allow for suffrage reform to be achieved by special laws. This open suffrage article would allow the Liberal Unionists to work for universal manhood suffrage and the Liberal Democrats to agitate for the vote to be universally given to men and women. The Old Liberals refused to sign this common election platform. At the same time the Left Opposition in Parliament, the Liberals and the Socialists, were united in their hatred for the Prime Minister and his cabinet. But the governing Right Coalition, the Anti-Revolutionaries and Catholics, supported by Christian Historicals, held fast. Kuyper still held considerable power as Prime Minister, Anti-Revolutionary Party chairman and Editor of *The Standard* even though he was inactive in the two latter posts. There was also tension within the Anti-Revolutionary Party. A.P. Staalman, M.P. for Den Helder, joined the Opposition because he felt the Prime Minister had reneged on his commitment to work actively for social reform legislation. Staalman began to organize his own progressive Christian Democratic Party.

The main campaign issues were: (1) for or against Kuyper, (2) political antithesis or neutrality, and (3) suffrage reform.

As the election grew more heated, the Anti-Revolutionary Party Congress convened in Utrecht on April 13, 1905. Kuyper chose not to attend since he was head of government. In his place Prof. Herman Bavinck was elected chairman of the party Central Committee. Prof. Bavinck, an internationally known Reformed theologian, taught at the Free University of Amsterdam and was the author of *The Doctrine of God* and *Our Reasonable Faith*.

After all the proper introductory statements were completed, Dr. Bavinck went to the podium to deliver a stirring speech on "Christian and Neutral Politics." He began with a strong endorsement of Kuyper's leadership. With his unusual talents, Kuyper had articulated party principles for over thirty years. What the Anti-Revolutionary party had become, Bavinck emphasized, was due to Kuyper's vigorous leadership. For such dynamic Christian leadership in party and state thanks must be given to God. But the ultimate basis of party unity was not a personality but a common commitment to principles.

Bavinck then engaged in a vigorous defense of the Kuyper government. The campaign of 1905 would be even more bitterly contested than that of 1901. Four years ago, the Liberals had acted as if the Anti-Revolutionaries did not exist; now they would make every effort to regain their former supremacy. Bavinck praised the high standards of ministerial competence and the accomplishments of the Kuyper Administration. The twenty-two governmental bills presented to Parliament, Bavinck affirmed, were concerned with the spiritual and material aspects of the social question. Governmental reforms had been founded upon the Christian basis of society.

The collective memory of the delegates was then refreshed concerning the details of the great railroad

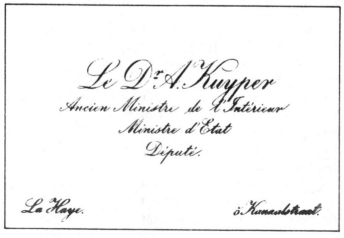

Kuyper's calling card (Documentatiecentrum, Vrije Universiteit te Amsterdam courtesy of its director, Dr. George Puchinger).

strike of 1903. Bavinck deplored the fact that some Liberals had supported the anarchist strikers in opposing the government, and he praised Kuyper's vigorous response to the strike both in Parliament and in the country at large. Bavinck saw in the strike and the anarchistic protests an attempt to intimidate the Kuyper Cabinet by a show of force. He called it shameful that certain Liberals publically refused to support the government on this matter.

Bavinck applauded the Higher Education Law of 1905 which put public and private universities on an equal academic footing. Likewise he supported the government's concern to improve the subsidies to private primary schools. The governmental bills on various social reforms including accident insurance for fishermen and farmers, technical education, regulation of labor contracts and protection against unfair industrial competition were cited to demonstrate that the government was not reactionary. The revised Liquor Law of 1904 was also seen as a practical piece of reform legislation.

According to Bavinck, "Down with the clericals, down with the Christian Cabinet, down with Kuyper," was the slogan of the Opposition. The Liberal-Socialist call for suffrage reform was based upon popular sovereignty which was different from suffrage reform based upon an organic view of society. But the deeper opposition to the Kuyper Cabinet, Bavinck emphasized, was a secularist rejection of its Christian basis. The opposition spoke of "neutral politics" over against Kuyper's politics of antithesis. A recent secularist manifesto had criticized the Kuyper Administration for mixing religion with politics, thereby profaning religion, curtailing liberty, and promoting divisiveness. Such opponents favored supporting Socialists rather than the Christian parties in the election. In Bavinck's view, these neutralists had no concern to conserve the Christian societal foundations or to work for reforms on a normative basis. They looked upon orthodox Christians as reactionary obscurantists while presenting Liberals as cultured progressives. "Our conduct," Bavinck carefully proclaimed, "must be based on principles which transcend base opportunism." While acknowledging that the modernist world-view was partially the borrowed capital of Christianity, he maintained that it was rooted, religiously, in Enlightenment unbelief, revolution, Hegelian rationalism, positivism, evolutionism, Marxist historical materialism, socialism, communism and anarchism. "Whoever fails to see this danger that threatens all of culture," Bavinck declared, "is blind. Everywhere in all civilized countries, among all Christian peoples, this struggle is the order of the day . . . The contest between belief and unbelief is the theme of world history." Pretended neutrality, the theologian charged, led to the dominance of unbelief and the undermining of the religious and ethical basis of society. Under the guise of neutrality, unbelief transformed the public school into a sectarian school of the modernist faith, while repressing the believing populace in the name of liberty.

The Christian concept of antithesis, a burning campaign issue, became the next focus of Bavinck's remarks. The Mackay and Kuyper Cabinets, based on the antithesis, had done more to preserve the Christian foundations of society than had all the previous Liberal governments put together, and they had also done more for Christian education and for the poor. Bavinck then turned to deeper matters. Man cannot live by bread alone. The Gospel of Christ is the believer's greatest treasure, and the Kingdom of Heaven is a pearl of great price. The Christian religion is not neutral between truth and falsehood. "Neither Groen van Prinsterer nor our party," Bavinck reminded the deputies, "accepted the separation of church and state in the sense that the state had no relation to God. Our Program of Principles states that in public life we confess the eternal principles of God's Word and the obligation of the government to be the servant of God in a Christian nation to glorify God's name." Governmental action must be based upon the ethical stance which religious faith provides for such matters as marriage laws, criminal law and Sunday legislation. Echoing a recent decision of the Reformed Churches of the Netherlands which revised Article 36 of the Belgic Confession, Bavinck emphasized that Christians, respecting freedom of conscience and of religious expression, must reject spiritual (theocratic) repression. Therefore, Christian principles applied toward a pluralist society had universal validity, providing a spiritual direction to be worked out in various situations. Bavinck refused to make an idol of patriotism as Kaiser Wilhelm II had done in Germany. "We dream of no seventeenth century restoration and even less of a millennial kingdom. Yet we have great courage." Bavinck ended by urging his hearers to vote for the Christian and truly Netherlandic cabinet.

Under Chairman Bavinck's leadership, the Congress then passed a resolution declaring that the Staalman group could not be considered party members while they were attempting to set up another political organization.

The Anti-Revolutionary delegates returned home from Utrecht with Bavinck's encouraging words of inspiration ringing in their ears.

In the June elections the Anti-Revolutionaries lost nine seats, winning only 15. The Right received a total of 48 seats. The Liberals received 45 and the Socialists 7, giving the Left a total of 52 seats. The vote was so close that if 199 more votes had been cast for the governing Right coalition in several districts, the final outcome would have been reversed. The defection of the Staalman group had also contributed to the poor Anti-Revolutionary showing at the polls.

The Kuyper Administration resigned in August. Abraham Kuyper, hoping to be recalled to office, left the country to travel around the Mediterranean for a year. He recorded his impressions of Palestine and other areas of the Middle East in his *Around the Old World Sea*.

In Holland the new Prime Minister was Th. de Meester who presided over a weak Left cabinet comprised of Liberal Unionists and Liberal Democrats. Prime Minister De Meester's main concern was a revision of the Constitution which would create a blank article allowing universal suffrage to be introduced. But in December, 1907, the De Meester Cabinet lost a crucial vote of confidence on the defense budget because the Right felt that the cabinet's military strategy had pacifistic overtones at a time when Europe seemed to be moving towards war. In the Second Chamber, the Liberal government received 38 votes and the Right gave 53 in opposition.

During the governmental crisis that followed, Kuyper was alone in hoping that he would be asked to form a second cabinet. In February, 1908, Queen Wilhelmina appointed the Anti-Revolutionary parliamentary leader Theodorus Heemskerk to head the new government. Prime Minister Heemskerk, the son of the major Conservative prime minister of the late nineteenth century, Jan Heemskerk, formed a cabinet of Anti-Revolutionary, Catholic and non-party ministers.

Party Tensions

Upon returning to Holland from his extended vacation, Kuyper resumed his journalistic work as editor of *The Standard* and prepared for a political come-back. While generally supporting the Heemskerk Administration, Kuyper sometimes criticized the new prime minister for not stating the political antithesis clearly enough. The allegiance of the party faithful was somewhat divided between Heemskerk and Kuyper. In addition, leaders of a new generation were coming into positions of influence within the party, such as Prime Minister Heemskerk, Rev. A.S. Talma, the Minister of Agriculture, Industry and Trade; the parliamentarians V.H. Rutgers and J. de Waal Malefijt as well as the Free University professors P.A. Diepenhorst and A. Anema. These younger leaders did not oppose Kuyper directly but acted independently at times. Another source of intraparty tension was the law professor D.P.D. Fabius who had been secretary of the party's Central Committee since 1879. Since 1903, Fabius had felt that Kuyper's political line was too progressive and thus "soft" on Liberals and Socialists. Fabius continued to write critical articles on this matter in an Anti-Revolutionary dissident daily, *The Rotterdammer*, charging that Kuyper emphasized organizational matters over principles. But Kuyper was again elected party chairman when Bavinck retired the post in October, 1907.

Kuyper then decided to deal with the tensions within the party by writing a series of unsigned articles on "Party Organization" published in *The Standard* between April 10 and 24, 1908. It was in 1903, the editorialist began, when the latest group of critics began to express some dissatisfaction with the line of the party congresses and the Central Committee. The malcontents in Naarden but especially in Groningen had called for a revision of the party constitution. In addition, *The Rotterdammer* was suspicious not only of the recent party congresses but also of its former chairman (Kuyper). The editorialist did not take the Rotterdam daily seriously, he said, since Kuyper was re-elected chairman by a vote of 733 to 13 at the special party congress held in Amsterdam on October 17, 1907. But he quickly added that the Central Committee itself favored a revision of the party constitution. All the Anti-Revolutionary papers were loyal except for *The Rotterdammer* and another small paper, *Our Journal*. While the malcontents were few in numbers, the editorialist admitted that they were having a negative influence on thousands of the Anti-Revolutionary rank-and-file. He acknowledged that every political party experienced tensions due to differences of opinion, but maintained that the Anti-Revolutionary party had experienced fewer tensions in the thirty years since its organization than other parties. The split in 1894 was hardly a schism since less than 300 members had resigned from Anti-Revolutionary voter's clubs. A few well-known aristocrats such as Jonkheer A.F. de Savornin Lohman and Jonkheer D.J. de

Geer had given visibility to the split. But the Christian Historical party was made up mostly of people who never were with the Anti-Revolutionaries. Indeed, this schism had strengthened the parties of the Right.

The editorialist reduced the current controversy to this question which he asked his readers: Do you want a party organization based upon the Christian wisdom of the common believers (upon "instinctive life") or upon man-centered study and reflection? He accused the critics of wanting to introduce a Liberal elitist idea of party organization into the Anti-Revolutionary Party. In the editorialist's view, such a trend would destroy the party's distinctiveness. Then he criticized the parties based on intellectual reflection: the Old Liberals and the Liberal Unionists as intellectually elitist, the Free Liberals and Socialists as intellectually proletarian. He praised the Catholic party for being a multi-class people's party based upon simple Christian wisdom, even if Romanist. The clear implication was that the Anti-Revolutionary Party alone was a proper multi-class people's party based on a proper sense of wisdom (instinctive life). He noted that Groen van Prinsterer with all his reformational insight and vision was unable to organize his co-religionists. In the 1860s and 70s he did attempt to give his advice to a small group of his aristocratic followers at election time and he did engage in some newspaper journalism and campaign pamphleteering. But he had only a vague idea of his influence among the Calvinist commoners. Nevertheless, Groen believed that simple Christians understood the basic problems facing believers better than did professional lawyers. The editorialist argued that the growth of the party began in 1871 when Groen endorsed L.W.C. Keuchenius, M.D. Van Otterloo and Kuyper as independent Anti-Revolutionary candidates for parliament. Without reference to anyone, but with Kuyper clearly in mind, the writer asserted that only then did the Calvinist revival and party formation take place. The commoners responded in large numbers to the Anti-Revolutionary

Program of Principles first published in 1878. The voter's clubs, provincial committees, Central Committee and parliamentary caucus were gradually established. Finally there were 1,000 delegates attending the party congresses. The editorial stressed the requirement that parliamentary candidates endorsed the party principles and current platform, even though freedom of conscience and minor differences were deemed appropriate for caucus members. The Central Committee promoted party unity, while the local independence of the voter's clubs was to be respected. The writer strongly affirmed that the decisions the party congress made before every national election, especially those of the action platform, were made after full discussion with both the voter's clubs and the delegates.

The editorialist concluded that King Saul was the man of technical reflection. But David, the man of wisdom (instinctive life), rejected the king's weapons when he went to fight Goliath in the name of the Lord. While there was a place for Christian reflection, the Anti-Revolutionary Party in its formation, action, struggle and goals could be understood only in terms of the higher significance of this mysterious wisdom.

Such articles in *The Standard*, undoubtedly by Kuyper himself, did help the leader in his attempt at a come-back. After Prime Minister Heemskerk made some strong statements affirming the antithesis, Kuyper decided to return to active politics. He defeated former Prime Minister De Meester in a parliamentary by-election in Ommen in late 1908. Immediately he became the chairman of the party's caucus in the Second Chamber.

Election of 1909

A number of political controversies set the stage for the election of 1909. In 1907 the Old Liberals finally organized themselves nationally as the Free Liberal Party, united in the conviction that the parliamentary First Chamber should restrain the agitation to widen the vote.

Then in July, 1908, several groups of Christian Historicals and Free Anti-Revolutionaries united to form the Christian Historical Union based on an articulation of the antithesis more muted than Kuyper's. Tensions within the Socialist movement reached a crisis in February, 1909, at the Deventer congress of the Social Democratic Workers' Party. The reformist majority led by M.W.F. Treub and P.J. Troelstra were successful in expelling the Marxist minority of D.J. Wijnkoop, the editor of *The Tribune*. The Social Democratic paper of Troelstra, *The People*, had frequently been criticized as bourgeois reformist by the revolutionary *Tribune*. The ousted Wijnkoop then founded a small Marxist party.

During the first months of 1909, the campaign was taking shape with parties either for or against the new Right coalition government. The Anti-Revolutionaries met in Utrecht on April 22, 1909 to hold the scheduled party congress. As Central Committee chairman, Kuyper delivered an address entitled "We Calvinists." As he spoke, the fact that 1909 marked the four hundredth anniversary of the birth of John Calvin was very much on his mind.

Kuyper began by acknowledging that the 1905 narrow defeat at the polls was a disappointment for the party as well as a source of personal frustration for him. He had been hurt by the intensely personal and abusive campaign waged against him by the Liberals, and had needed an extended vacation after retiring from office.

He brought the question of tactics to the center of attention. Since the party would probably never have a majority of elected parliamentarians, it had two choices: either (1) to be a small protest party or (2) to join a larger coalition in order to take part in the government at appropriate times. Kuyper then declared that in 1874 Groen van Prinsterer had personally advised him to adopt the second option by seeking to cooperate with the Catholics in order to provide an alternative to unending Liberal rule. Groen had tried the first option in Parliament, protesting for many years, but then the situation had changed. "From that moment on," Kuyper declared, "I began to build the coalition. This coalition then became a reality." The cooperation of Anti-Revolutionaries, Christian Historicals and Catholics was possible because of their unity of faith in the Kingship of Christ and in the trustworthy character of Scripture. Each of these parties worked out this common faith in different ways according to their traditions. But there was unity enough to form a government. Kuyper warned the party faithful not to be too critical of the Heemskerk coalition government. All men are fallible, he said, and criticism must be offered in a spirit of brotherhood. He then sought to clarify the nature of the coalition: it was a federation to achieve a limited set of common political goals; it was not a fusion of the confessional parties. In no way did Kuyper favor the amalgamation of the Protestant and Catholic parties. He urged the Anti-Revolutionaries to be faithful to their Calvinist principles, which had implications for every area of life. He stated three basic rules of conduct: (1) as Calvinists, the Anti-Revolutionaries confessed the principles articulated within their own party; (2) then they cooperated with other confessional parties; (3) being a part of a coalition did not hinder the development of Anti-Revolutionary Party independence.

Kuyper then declared that the antithesis between would-be autonomous man and man subject to scriptural normativity and the sovereign Christ was the basic dividing line for life and politics in the modern age. Groen's slogan "The Gospel versus the Revolution" was an appropriate statement of this fundamental clash of principles. "The antithesis," he added, "is the cement which holds the coalition together." The disharmony caused by the antithesis was not a human innovation; Christ Himself gave it to distinguish the saved from the lost. But the Liberals, since the days of Groen, in their general hatred of Calvinists, and in the campaign of 1905, had tried to deny the existence of the antithesis because the popular masses were being made aware of it. In response, the Liberals had accused the confessional parties of sowing discord among the people.

The clearest expression of the biblical antithesis was to be found in the Calvinist tradition. The chairman noted that historically there was a positive relationship between Calvinism and constitutional liberties in Holland, Scotland and America. Of the three main streams of Dutch history (Catholic, Calvinist and secularist), the Calvinism which had formed the Netherlandic nation in the sixteenth century had been undergoing a revival since 1850. Reformed Christians were seeking to obey God's cultural mandate to honor Him in all areas of life; they were recognizing that God's common revelation can be seen in nature, history and conscience when viewed from the normative vantage point of His scriptural Word. In the modern age, the Calvinist tradition can be applied freed from its theocratic elements. Kuyper ended his speech with an appeal for the party to be faithful to the main ideas of Calvin's thought: the struggle to honor God in every endeavor and to work for the realization of popular freedoms. After Kuyper left the podium, the enthusiastic delegates were soon on the way home to participate in the final weeks of the campaign.

The election results were an unqualified victory for the Right coalition of Prime Minister Heemskerk. The parties of the Right won 60 seats (up from 48 in 1905) of which 25 went to Anti-Revolutionaries (a gain of 10 from 1905). The Left received only 40 seats.

But during the campaign Kuyper became involved in the "decoration affair" which dragged on for another year. A Liberal spokesman at Ommen (where Kuyper held his seat) charged that Kuyper had been involved in financial corruption as prime minister. It seems that in 1903 a Jewish businessman from Amsterdam, R. Lehman, had been greatly impressed with the Prime Minister's strong law-and-order policy in dealing with the railroad strike. On Kuyper's recommendation, Queen Wilhelmina made Lehman an officer in the Order of Orange-Nassau. At about the same time Lehman donated a large sum of money (perhaps $5,000) to the Anti-Revolutionary campaign fund. As Kuyper left office, Lehman's brother was being considered for a similar decoration. After being attacked for corruption by the Socialist leader Troelstra, Kuyper admitted in November, 1909, that perhaps he had not exercised sufficient good judgment in the affair. But in his view, Lehman had deserved the decoration he was awarded. Kuyper then requested an *ad hoc* parliamentary committee with a Left majority to look into the matter. In July, 1910, the *ad hoc* committee declared Kuyper to be innocent of any financial corruption in the "decoration affair." Nevertheless, the "decoration affair" contributed to a lessening of Kuyper's national prestige. During the period from 1905 to 1910, Kuyper experienced the painful transition from chief executive of the nation to elder statesman respected only by the parties of the Right.

Comments

1. Kuyper paid a price for his years of national influence and power. He had the satisfaction of having insured the long-term existence of a pluralist system which included a place for Christian influence. But he also suffered the defeat of 1905, a continuing hate campaign against him, and the personal stigma of the "decoration affair." It is often impossible for national political leaders to escape the scars of battle. As Herbert Hoover remarked after suffering defeat in the presidential campaign of 1932, "Democracy is not a polite employer."

2. The tensions within the Anti-Revolutionary Party were partially due to Kuyper's strong leadership and the individualism of others. His government was too Christian for some, while not Christian enough for others. Sometimes Kuyper identified himself too closely with the

party and its principles, causing dissatisfaction among other members.

3. The decision to create a working coalition between the Anti-Revolutionary, Christian Historical and Catholic parties made possible the coming to power of the Right cabinets of Mackay, Kuyper and Heemskerk between 1888 and 1907. As architect of this coalition, Kuyper never wanted an ecumenical synthesis between Protestants and Catholics. Instead, he envisioned an alliance of co-belligerents, an alternative to the secularist parties, to achieve specific goals. Kuyper had made the point in *The Standard* as early as the 1870s that this cooperation was limited to achieving common goals. Anti-Revolutionaries supported equal rights for all groups including Catholics, therefore the cooperation was on issues such as the school question and pluralist reformism. In employing a co-belligerency tactic with the Catholics, Kuyper also stressed common Christian beliefs in distinction from the beliefs of the secularist parties (for more details see *The Standard* of April 5, 1873; June 1, 1875 and July 7, 1875). But Kuyper clearly rejected any notion of a united political party of Protestants and Catholics. Under his leadership, the Anti-Revolutionary Party maintained its Reformed confessional integrity and general political independence.

4. Reference to the difference between Christian wisdom (instinctive life) and reflection was perhaps an early form of the naive-theoretical distinction articulated by reformational philosophy.

5. Understanding the debate whether antithesis or neutrality is the basis of public life is fundamental if one wishes to discern the religious direction of modern life in the Western world. The Liberals and Socialists always resisted Kuyper's heroic attempt to realign public affairs either for or against the cosmic implications of the Gospel of Christ. Kuyper's basic conviction was that life is either lived in subjection to the normative character of Scripture or according to the shifting opinions of would-be

autonomous man. The antithesis, as Kuyper and Bavinck courageously declared, cuts through every aspect of life. The notion of a neutral or objective view of culture, politics and scholarship, a view which is the cornerstone of modern(ist) thought, is based upon the false assumption that man can finally know ultimate truth without God and without acknowledging sin. But only the antithesis position properly takes into account human sin and the need for scriptural revelation of basic truth.

Kuyper on the 40th anniversary of his editorship of *The Standard* in 1912 (Documentatiecentrum, Vrije Universiteit te Amsterdam courtesy of its director, Dr. George Puchinger).

Chapter 14

A Practical Statesman with a Theological Background

"*I* AM NOT A LAWYER, NEITHER BY TALENT nor by study. The honorary doctorates I have received in Political Science from Princeton University in the United States and in Laws from the Catholic University of Louvain, Belgium, have not changed me. I remain a practical statesman with a theological background. Any other stamp would be incorrect that is put on the present study that I offer only to co-religionists, as I did my earlier book, *Our Program*." These autobiographical words were penned by Elder Statesman Abraham Kuyper to preface his two-volume work, *Anti-Revolutionary Political Science* published during the latter half of 1916. In spite of his long and successful political career, he wanted his readers to remember that he had not given the last word on political science. He was, he confessed, ". . . a practical statesman with a theological background." Nevertheless, during his last years Kuyper reflected deeply on the meaning of Christians living in a secular world, a world which included the realm of public affairs.

Elder Statesman

Even as early as his coming to power in 1901, Kuyper began to assume the role of Elder Statesman. He began to publish a number of volumes containing his mature reflections on the meaning of Christian life in a secular world. *Common Grace*, originally an extended series of articles in *The Herald*, was published in three big volumes between 1902 and 1904. The three important volumes comprising *Pro Rege or the Kingship of Christ*, another *Herald* series, were published between 1911 and 1912. Finally, the two volumes of *Anti-Revolutionary Political Science* saw the light of day in 1916-1917 as part of a commentary on the revised Anti-Revolutionary Program of Principles. Taken together, the Kuyperian insights in these eight thick volumes sum up what his vast political experience had meant to this man of God. He offered a theological perception of the meaning of secular modernity, full of implications for politics. Kuyper was unable to give a lawyer's analysis of statecraft or a philosopher's theory of political science; he was aware that he could not do everything. What does emerge in Kuyper's volumes is a revitalized understanding and application of both common grace and the Kingship of Christ for all of life. Kuyper's great contribution was to give Christians a sense of religious direction in private and public matters. In this sense the Elder Statesman was a visionary whose message has great relevance for our own day. Kuyper wanted to restore religious unity to the thought and life of Christians.

Common Grace

Common grace is the way God acts toward all men. The rain falls on the just and the unjust. In a general sense, God restrains the full out-working of the disastrous results of sin while giving to various individuals and groups positive abilities to make progress. In reviving the old dogma of common grace, Kuyper was trying to eliminate the one-sided spirituality embraced by many Christians. Both the struggle for Christian schools, begun by Groen van Prinsterer, and the problems Christian workers had getting suitable jobs had highlighted the problems Christians face outside the institutional churches. Quite correctly the Reformed confession begins with the absolute sovereignty of the Lord Creator and Redeemer. Mankind has been given a mandate to subdue the earth for God's glory. Jesus prayed not that believers would be taken from the world but that they would be protected from the Evil One in the world. "In the midst of the world is our calling," Kuyper declared, "and here must the Lord our God be glorified."

Put very simply, the church is the domain of special grace, and the civic, non-ecclesiastical area is the domain of common grace. God created government to restrain the social effects of man's sin. Government, outside the realm of special revelation, includes all people. Common grace is the basis for the institution of the state, the foundation of its conduct, and provides the band of conscience between the state and the people. The idea of civic law is strengthened by tradition, history and genius. God works in history. The foundation for the state is seen in the law of capital punishment and public justice in Genesis 9 and Romans 13. With Noah, God made a covenant of common grace, and even the heathens have some distorted knowledge of it. Government is always God's servant for blessing or curse. Rulers must not use the Bible as a textbook for political science, for the Old Testament theocracy has expired and God no longer rules His people directly. But public authorities are called to uphold God's common grace law in the midst of the people as well as to regulate the relations between men in the light of that law. The innate popular consciousness of honesty, law and the honoring of the state is to be encouraged by responsible leadership and administration.

Common grace is based on the realities of creation. Thus it is necessary to maintain the independence of social groups from the centralizing tendencies of the modern state; life is more than politics. The Creator has delegated aspects of His authority to all the diverse social spheres of life. We have a mandate, Kuyper affirmed, to use our influence in this life because through Christ, God made the world. Even creation has an original tie to

Christ. Upon this earthly terrain, God has made Christ the Heir of all things. The Christian belongs to both creation and recreation; in both we must fulfill our calling. Work was basic to life even before the fall into sin. Common grace retards sin, and thereby makes social life and progress possible.

Pro Rege

Secularization, Kuyper pointed out perceptively, has obliterated any national consciousness of the Kingship of Jesus. Unbelievers influence believers more deeply all the time. Christians, in reaction, flee into mystical isolation. But not only in a limited spiritual area, Kuyper declared boldly, but in the entire sweep of human life, the Kingship of Christ must be given its due. With such firm conviction, Kuyper raised again the majestic biblical task of living comprehensively *Pro Rege* — for the King.

Kuyper was unflinching in his challenge: "He who really accepts Jesus as his Savior and glories in his calling to eternal life but unconditionally omits coming to the conclusion that Christ is *his Lord, his King*, his complete *Commander* and the absolute *Controller* over his destiny and life, runs great danger of making his own name unreadable in the book of life."

The royal dominion of Christ is three-fold: (1) over the sphere of believers in which Christ is the Head of His Body; (2) over the sphere of the unsaved world in which He is the Judge; and (3) over the sphere of the good and evil spirits of which He is Lord. The Father gave Jesus the Kingship over the Kingdom of God. As the Second Person of the Trinity, He possesses kingly rule in His own right. This Kingdom is in constant spiritual warfare with the forces of darkness. Dualistic separation of the sacred from the profane is false and misleading, for the dominion of Christ is total, all-inclusive: "The royal dominion of Christ is not limited to your spiritual life. It presses in on all the orders and stages of the creation." Christ is the Preserver of His Body and of the world which will be changed into the new heaven and the new earth. The bodily resurrection of Christ and finally of all believers demonstrates that Kingship is not limited to the spiritual. The Kingdom brings life. "From life comes the grace-movement."

The unfolding of the Kingdom happens in four stages. The first was the preparation, from paradise to the coming of John the Baptist. The second stage was the foundation of the Kingdom, from the birth of Christ in Bethlehem to His Ascension from the Mount of Olives. The third stage is the practice of the Kingdom in world history, from the Cross to the Second Coming. During this important third period, Christian enterprise is necessary. The fourth and final stage is the consummation of the Kingdom with the Second Coming of Christ. The eternal Kingdom will be the final glorification of believers and of the creation.

The essence of Kingship is found within the circle of the born-again believers: "This circle which forms the center of Jesus' dominion is a human circle; it is not the circle of merely one people." The Body of Christ is organic in character and is saved as a unit. Like the vine and the branches, Christ is the Head of the Body in both a spiritual and a material sense. Rebirth by grace, the gift of personal and heart-felt faith in Christ, is the key to entering the Kingdom. Then the people of God have a Kingdom-task to perform: "In all relations of general human life He must have influence. In a long, hard struggle, the members of the Body of Christ must spiritually win the world for Him. All the treasures, all the talents which God created in our human race and which have come to fruition, must sanctify the Name of Christ." The visible church (Gemeente) is the bodyguard of Christ. It is only in the church that His royal honor and majesty not only work but are recognized and praised. But the royal majesty of Christ extends far beyond the visible church. Kuyper confessed, "In the place satan occupied, now Christ is the Lord and Master of our hearts. We now belong to Him with body and soul, with all our person, abilities and gifts. Not for ourselves but for Him we exist, live, suffer and bear responsibilities. This is now the deep meaning and significance of what is involved when we call Christ *our Lord*."

We lose ourselves in Him and win the full freedom of the children of God. Our servanthood involves both the renunciation of self-will and, as soldiers of the Lord, giving all courage, strength and enthusiasm in following the directives of the divine Field Marshal. The Messiah has restored God's spiritual dominion over all nations disturbed as they are by sin. With the destruction of the Old Testament Jewish theocracy and the coming of the Messiah, the special task for earthly Israel came to an end. Israel is now a nation like all the other nations of the world. This is the teaching of the parable of the Vineyard. Since evil men killed the Heir, the Vineyard has been given to others. But there is more. "His royal dominion is grounded in the creation of all things by the

The inner reformation: Kuyper in his study at home in The Hague (Documentatiecentrum, Vrije Universiteit te Amsterdam courtesy of its director, Dr. George Puchinger).

Eternal Word and permeates all spheres of creation. In the end nothing in heaven or earth will be left out of this royal dominion." The Beast of the Book of Revelation is a picture of depraved mankind throughout the ages, mankind who has descended to the level of animals. For without God's ordinances for all of life, the demonic world would finally conquer all higher elements in man and reduce him to a dehumanized, bestial existence. Death, not sin, is the final enemy that the King will conquer.

After this long discussion of the majestic and universal implications of the King and His Kingdom, Kuyper ended by quietly calling for more preaching and meditation on the profound implications of the gracious conversion of the sinner to the Lord Christ. (In our terms: "Jesus loves me; this I know, for the Bible tells me so.") The coming of the Father of Spirits to the spirit of man is, in a nutshell, the work of revelation. Ending with meditation upon the love of God, Kuyper wrote with deep reverence and thankfulness: "The Kingdom is of the King. Preaching begins not with the Savior but with the emphasis on the King. This King will bring salvation to the nations and everything to the higher glory."

Further Experience

In June of 1916 the distinguished elder statesman sat down in his booklined study to compose the introduction to *Anti-Revolutionary Political Science*. His thoughts returned to his younger days as a theological student at Leiden University and his personal spiritual struggle with modernism and the meaning of Reformation history. John Calvin, John Knox, the Pilgrim Fathers in Massachusetts and Groen van Prinsterer all came to mind. He recalled his coming as pastor to the New Church in Amsterdam in 1870 and the many cordial contacts with Groen during that period which were so important for his own development. He remembered that in 1870 Calvinism had almost no influence in the universities. He must have been thankful that since that time there had been a great spiritual awakening in many aspects of national life.

Governmental authority, he remembered, was rooted in the conscience, in history and in the necessity for an ordered society. The fall into sin with its dehumanizing consequences made the state necessary for maintaining law and order, beginning with the rule of capital punishment for premeditated murder. The authority of government has divine sanction. The state must cut out injustice with the sword of justice, retarding social evil and promoting civil goodness. And yet politics and the state are only parts of life. God has given separate and limited sovereignties to the other aspects of life so that God-given mandates may be fulfilled in the family, the church, in scholarship, art, trade, industry, agriculture and many organizations and groups. While the state must keep order in society, it must not swallow up these other spheres. This idea, Kuyper called "sphere sovereignty." Kuyper also defended his strategy of building a working political coalition with the Catholic political party, a strategy pursued since the days of his first election to Parliament from Gouda in 1874. This coalition strategy produced the Anti-Revolutionary Prime Ministers Mackay in 1888, Kuyper in 1901 and Heemskerk in 1908. While sharp ecclesiastical and theological differences divided Calvinists and Catholics, politically they stood together against the humanist parties and achieved common goals such as the introduction of a multi-party system and pluralist education.

Kuyper dealt with a number of other matters which should be noted briefly. He believed Sunday to be a common grace day of rest and not specifically Christian. While basically believing that businesses should be closed on Sunday, he pointed out that the police, fire departments, health services, public utilities, drugstores and the like could not cease their important and often vital tasks. State theaters were not to be open on Sunday. Kuyper expressed his objection to all lewd entertainment on the basis of his ". . . puritanical modesty." He also favored a common grace civic prayer (making reference only to God) to be used by public officials at the opening of legislative sessions. Yet in town councils where there was a large Christian population, he felt it was permissible to pray in the name of Christ. Kuyper also felt strongly about opposing immoral practices. He favored strict laws against divorce, declaring that the Liberals wanted to make divorce easier in order to popularize a liberated life. Likewise he spoke of prostitution as a great moral evil and public health problem. He was opposed to the legalization of brothels and sex traffic. He endorsed the continuance of capital punishment for premeditated murder, arguing on the basis of Genesis 9.

Finally Kuyper turned his attention to economics. He affirmed his commitment to a mixed economy in which private and public sectors work together. Some tasks could best be done by private companies while other responsibilities were best handled by the state. Private businesses were to be regulated by the government to insure that they did not engage in exploitation. For example, he favored private railroad companies which were carefully regulated by the state to prevent massive strikes, such as the Great Strike of 1903, which crippled the nation. He spoke with profound awareness of the problems between capital and labor concerning wages, factory conditions, job security, unemployment and organizations of both workers and employers. Kuyper maintained that public regulation of both industrial concerns and labor unions was necessary to ensure the rights of both. Concerning that most serious labor problem, unemployment, Kuyper thought that government should take partial responsibility for the jobless by requiring private companies to sign collective labor contracts with the labor unions and by introducing unemployment insurance. Kuyper rejected an absolute *laissez faire* economy, believing that it hurt and demoralized workers. Rejecting a class-struggle model, he advocated a cooperation model between management and labor to settle disputes.

Comments

1. Kuyper's greatest contribution as an elder statesman was his practical vision. His perspective on the world was both profound and simple. His major books of the later period, books on common grace, the Kingship of Christ, and politics kept returning to a few basic concepts. The hundreds of pages of these books are often repetitive. Repetition was Kuyper's teaching method; because of it, readers in large numbers were able to grasp his main points. On the other hand, Kuyper could also talk around most anything without saying very much that was new or helpful. Some of these books could have said as much in half as many pages. But since most of Kuyper's books were originally long series of newspaper articles, the repetition is again understandable. Through a clutter of words and a mountain of paper, the Kuyperian vision shines forth. Therein lies the Elder Statesman's lasting influence.

2. Kuyper's basic position laid foundations for later refinements by philosophers, historians, lawyers, political scientists and theologians. Kuyper openly admitted that he was not a lawyer and that there was much he did not know about politics. Yet because of his significant political experience, he could rightly consider himself a practical statesman. He was more than an ivory tower theorist. His ideas had been tested in the rough-and-tumble world of public affairs. That he did construct the groundwork for dealing with the problem of Christians in a secular world cannot be ignored. Much work on Kuyper's contribution to a Christian view of culture and political spirituality still needs to be done.

3. It was crucially important that Kuyper articulated the significance of common grace and the Kingdom of God as the rationale for his sustained activities outside the institutional church. Common grace checks the outworking of sin and enables society to function and make pro-

gress. God deals with all men with such grace. The state is an instrument of common grace just as the church is the sphere of saving grace. Christ rules as Lord over the saved and as Judge over the unredeemed world and evil spirits. Common grace preserves temporal life everywhere while the Kingdom invades the world for Christ. By appealing to the reality of common grace, Kuyper could get involved in civic, cultural and educational matters. By believing in the present and future reality of the Kingdom of God, he created separate Christian organizations to witness to, and to extend the Kingdom. Therefore he could affirm both the commonality of human life and a sharp antithesis between belief and unbelief. Not all is crystal clear. There is a place for mystery in God's work, and there are also many blind spots in Kuyper's vision. Nevertheless, Kuyper showed afresh how great Christ is, in His creative power and His Gospel. Starting with the sovereignty of God and the new birth, Kuyper explored the larger dimensions of a faith which professes the cultural mandate, amillennialism, and the Kingdom-covenant. The result was the outline of a comprehensive Reformed alternative to those dualistic or secularistic viewpoints which have caused Christians to suffer great setbacks in the modern age as they struggle against the power of those who ignore the God of the heavens and the earth.

4. Kuyper himself was unable to articulate a systematic Christian theory of the state. He did not seem to have the mental concentration or the inclination to give the reading public the fruits of his own political career. Apparently he never wrote an autobiography. But with his comprehensive vision and intense spiritual power, he was able to inspire a small army of Christians to carry on the Kingdom tasks and reflection that he had begun in the 1860s. It is this vision of total service to the King in a broken and hostile world, this deep search for the meaning of the Gospel of Christ in our secular age that is the greatest legacy of Abraham Kuyper, elder statesman and servant of God.

With confidence he confessed: "In the place of satan, Christ is now the Lord and Master of our hearts" (Documentatiecentrum, Vrije Universiteit te Amsterdam courtesy of its director, Dr. George Puchinger).

Chapter 15

Final Statements

O N MARCH 30, 1914 *THE STANDARD* carried the obituary of Pietje Baltus, a believing woman in Dr. Abraham Kuyper's first pastoral charge, the country church at Beesd during the years 1863-1867. Miss Baltus had confronted the preacher with his own weak position and with the spiritual strength of the orthodox Calvinist heritage. Forever afterwards Dr. Kuyper had been thankful for her sense of the absolute majesty of God, a decisive confession which she had communicated to him. Another newspaper, *The Telegraph*, noted that because of her spiritual influence on Kuyper, Miss Baltus had significantly influenced national church history during the preceeding half century. The editorialist for *The Standard* urged his readers to carry on the glorious tradition of this humble woman's witness.

Behind all of Abraham Kuyper's accomplishments, there was a child of God with a mature spirituality firmly based on deep faith in the historic Christ of the Scriptures. In the last years of this great man's life, glimmers of this deep spirituality could be seen even in his final statements on behalf of the Anti-Revolutionary Party.

Pacification

The period from 1913 to 1918, when Kuyper made his final statements to the party faithful, was an eventful period for Holland and for Kuyper. In national politics, the Anti-Revolutionary Prime Minister, Theodorus Heemskerk, was defeated in the election of 1913 and replaced by Prime Minister P.W.A. Cort van der Linden who headed an extra-parliamentary Liberal coalition government until 1918. Anxious to end the years of political tension between the parties of the Right and the Left, Cort van der Linden introduced bills in Parliament providing for constitutional revisions in favor of complete educational pluralism and proportional representation. In 1917 both bills were passed into law by respectable majorities. The Pacification in education provided for public and private primary schools to be equally funded by public taxation. The electoral reform introduced proportional representation in which each one percent of the national vote would elect one candidate to the parliamentary Second Chamber. The whole country was to be considered one electoral district. The new law also provided for universal manhood suffrage and the nomination of parliamentary candidates by means of party voting lists. These constitutional revisions of 1917 marked a final legal victory for the social pluralism for which Kuyper had been fighting since 1869.

Physical Decline

As Anti-Revolutionary party leader, Kuyper gave his last four major speeches during this same period: "Maypole on the Roof" (April 24, 1913), "Root in the Dry Ground" (November 2, 1916), "The Little People" (November 23, 1917) and "What Now?" (May 2, 1918). His remarks reflected the situation in which the party and the nation found themselves. He attempted to give the membership a clear sense of their present and future responsibilities as he prepared them for a change in party leadership.

In 1913 Kuyper was 76 years old and starting to decline. A lifelong "workaholic," he began to find it difficult to keep up with his writing and party activities. In

December of 1916 and January of 1917 he began to suffer from influenza, bronchitis, recurring high temperatures, some serious falls, a loss of strength and a loss of his speaking voice. He completed his last book, *Anti-Revolutionary Political Science*, in 1916. He penned his last editorials for *The Standard* in December, 1919. On March 31, 1920 he resigned as party leader. By the early summer of 1920 he was unable to continue to write theological articles for *The Herald*. On September 21, 1920 he resigned his seat in the parliamentary First Chamber. Yet he continued to try to write his beloved meditations, finding great comfort in reading Scripture's promises of the final victory of Christ.

Three Speeches

The speeches, "Maypole on the Roof," "Root in the Dry Ground," and "The Little People," reflected some basic themes that occupied Kuyper's mind during this period. The first theme was his joy that after spending years in the wilderness of legal discrimination, the Christian schools had come out with full legal and financial equality. Having fought for this goal for more than fifty years, the old party leader now expressed his feeling in a restrained manner. Now, he said, the Maypole—the sign of victory—was symbolically put on the roof of this school of belief. Groen had worked for many years to lay the foundations for the Christian school movement during a period when Christians did not realize how important the movement would be for the future expression of Christian values. The first Anti-Revolutionary government of Prime Minister Mackay broke the power of the unbelieving Liberal oligarchy. Then came the period of success culminating in full equality for the Christian schools. The aging leader called for prayers of thankfulness to be given to God.

Another important theme in these speeches was that Kuyper called the great struggle between Christian belief and unbelieving secularity in European history. Since the

Reformation period, there had been a steady apostate
secularization of European culture. Kuyper noted, by way
of example, the drastic decrease in faithful church attendance. Quoting Isaiah 53:2, Kuyper declared that
spiritual reformation can come only from Christ, the root
in the dry ground of unbelief. He contrasted the false
wisdom of antiquity and of the French Revolution with
the saving truth of the Gospel of Christ, eulogizing
modern heroes of faith such as the historian Groen van
Prinsterer, the poet Willem Bilderdijk and the converted
Jew, Isaac da Costa. But above all Kuyper praised the
faith and tenacity of the *kleine luyden*, the believing commoners. These simple people of the rural areas had
formed the backbone of the Anti-Revolutionary movement in church and state during the preceeding half century. They went to church every Sunday, read their Bibles
at the table with their families, and supported the ad-
vancement of the cause of Christ.

The growth of the Anti-Revolutionary Party was the
final theme of these speeches. With justifiable pride,
Kuyper pointed out that at the first party congress in 1881
there were thirty delegates in attendance, representing six
voter's clubs. By 1905 there were 2,500 delegates
representing 640 voter's clubs. The old leader once again
gave his stamp of approval to the idea of a common election strategy between Anti-Revolutionaries, Christian
Historicals and Catholics. In this way, Christians had
presented a united front to the secularist parties without
doing more than agreeing upon a common strategy at the
polls. It was during this time that the Anti-Revolutionary
Party made some slight readjustments in its own principles and constitution in order to meet new problems,
while maintaining the clear Anti-Revolutionary confessional basis. Kuyper also took careful note of the constitutional victory establishing proportional representation.

Final Statement

Kuyper's final speech, entitled "What Now?" was delivered on May 2, 1918 at Utrecht. It was read by the party vice-chairman, A.W.F. Idenburg, since the aging chairman had just suffered a bad fall and had also lost his voice. This speech was remarkable because of the attention it paid to the future and not the past. Now that the school struggle was over, Kuyper asked, what was the party going to do? What now? His answer: the party must face the social problems of poverty, economic injustice and the plight of the workman. The notion of the state as night watchman is no longer adequate in the modern world. The state must take responsibility for insuring that society is really free and not bound to unscrupulous businessmen or the forces of violence and crime. The state must provide social insurance against accidents, illness, and retirement for workmen and pensions for widows and children. The day laborer must be taught a sense of social responsibility. Anti-Revolutionary politics in the future, Kuyper wrote, must put a high priority on solving social problems. Kuyper mentioned his largely unsuccessful efforts to introduce social legislation during his years in power in The Hague. The problems of refugees, scarce resources, and faltering trade, all caused by World War I, made this more of a priority for state intervention than ever before. Kuyper concluded by emphasizing that concern for the problems of labor did not arise from mere interest-group politics but a politics that sought to honor God in national life. The Christian labor unions played an important role in dealing with justice in jobs, wages and social insurance. Interdependence and a concern for economic justice were among Kuyper's final public thoughts presented to the party faithful.

Tribute

On November 8, 1920 the old Christian soldier went to be with his Savior. He had lived eighty-three years full

of pain, victories and Christian service. At his graveside
on November 12, the former Anti-Revolutionary prime
minister, Theodorus Heemskerk, speaking on behalf of
the Ruijs de Beerenbrouck Cabinet uttered the following
simple yet moving words which expressed the feelings of
many:

> Abraham Kuyper waged a struggle and completed a work as
> almost no one else was given to do as Minister of the Word,
> Church Reformer, University Founder, orator, publicist, a
> born leader, representative of the people and prime minister.
> As successor to Groen van Prinsterer, "Not a Statesman but a
> Gospel Confessor" was the secret of his vitality and of the
> Christian principle governing all of life in subjection to God's
> ordinances and giving unity in Church and State, in scholar-
> ship, in society and in personal life. In all of his diversity
> there was unity and a system. He was the bearer of the same
> principle in every area. He fought to bring stability to the
> constant changes in temporal life, never giving up the battle,
> yet seeking reconciliation with the various classes and social
> groups. He was the upholder of authority and a warrior ex-
> tending the influence of the people and revitalizing national
> spiritual life. Thus will his memory remain alive in the con-
> sciousness of the people with whom he deeply sympathized
> and to whom he has bequeathed a great and solemn calling
> and task . . .

Reflections

1. In his declining years Kuyper wanted the Anti-
Revolutionary Party to carry on with those tasks for the
Lord which Groen van Prinsterer had given him in the
1870s. His vision was of Christian witness and action ex-
tending from the Cross to the Second Coming. In his own
national situation he wanted public witness to be carried
out on a long-term basis. The attitude which grounded
his view of sanctification as applied to public affairs was
political spirituality. Christians must always maintain a
politically spiritual attitude towards society, regardless of
the success or failure of Christian action. The believer
must have a clear idea of what it means to be a Christian
in the secular world. For this reason, Kuyper kept return-

ing in his thought to Groen van Prinsterer's pioneering articulation of political spirituality.

2. In his declining years, Kuyper's memory dwelt on the beginning of his career and his formative relationship with Groen. The early struggles of the late 1860s and the 1870s were important to him as examples of the Lord's sustaining grace in the midst of discouragement and failure. The most important thing to Groen and Kuyper had been faithfulness. They had articulated an attitude of political spirituality as part of a total Christian reawakening in church and state when few people were paying much attention. Both men affirmed, quite rightly, that an attitude of truth before the Lord was more important than success.

3. Yet in the providence of God, Kuyper lived to see legal victory after his half-century struggle for true educational and political pluralism. His joy was real but subdued. Such victory was "icing on the cake" of public policy such as few Christian statesmen have ever lived to see. When he had finally seen the fruits of his politically spiritual faithfulness, he refrained from praising himself as the indispensable leader. Instead, he saw this success as a Christian communal work begun in the early nineteenth century.

4. In his final statement to the party, the old leader pointed the way to the future with a sense of vision, organization and a set of priorities. With courage, he faced the uncomfortable problems of poverty and economic injustice. At the end of his career as at the beginning of it, Kuyper made clear that he was not a conservative but a Protestant Christian Democrat with a distinctive set of principles, attitudes and concerns. The Anti-Revolutionary Party survived from 1879 to 1980. The spiritual key to a century of effective Christian witness was Kuyper's magnificent attitude of political spirituality. In every country and in every age, Christians must accept the responsibility to articulate a politically spiritual attitude toward society as part of their total con-

cern to live a sanctified life. The present writer hopes that as believers in various countries and situations consider their own attitudes toward society, they will examine the legacy of political spirituality left by Abraham Kuyper, a legacy which provides not the final word on Christian political action, but a basis for reflection and discussion.

Kuyper's Legacy

Chapter 16

The Legacy of Kuyper's Political Spirituality

*I*N THESE PAGES WE HAVE EXPLORED some concrete examples of Kuyper's politically spiritual attitude at work in various specific episodes throughout his long career. Now we must attempt to draw some lessons from his experience and see what contribution his legacy can make to the current discussion of born-again politics and the growing international awareness of the relation between self-conscious religious faith and public affairs.

A. Kuyper the Man

It is clear that Abraham Kuyper was an unusual Christian leader. He exercized great talents in many fields for half a century. His work as a journalist, statesman, public speaker, and educator required enormous energy and insight. It has been beyond the scope of this study to deal with his significant work as a theologian and a church leader. In all of these accomplishments he did the work of several men. But the man was exceptional not only because of his enormous energy. Kuyper was unusual because he developed a comprehensive vision of the Christian life in the modern secular world. In that sense he was building on the perspective inherited from Calvin's sixteenth century *Institutes of the Christian Religion* and even from Augustine's fifth century *City of God*. Augustine and Calvin made important statements about the comprehensive character of the kingdom of God and the task of believers in hostile pagan and apostate environments. Kuyper provided an updated version of this comprehensive Christian vision in our modern age of indifferent secularism. In this sense Kuyper can be rightfully termed one of the most important Christian thinkers and leaders of the modern period.

All of these great insights and enormous energies were incarnated in a typical nineteenth century "great leader." The gifted organizer and statesman was also a workaholic who was convinced that virtually he alone was right on many matters. His powerful critique of secularism and modernism was accompanied by a mixture of child-like humility and intolerant arrogance. Kuyper jealously guarded his power. His attitude was tender toward the common people but often harsh toward his peers. In unending debates with various enemies he was often abrasive and tactless. So convinced was he of his Christian cause of comprehensive witness and social emancipation that he tended to see criticism of his public conduct as criticism of Christian principles. His tenacity as leader of the Anti-Revolutionary Party through thick and thin was related to his inability to get along with other leaders; he had difficulty taking their criticism and suggestions for change with grace. Yet at the same time Kuyper had sensed the direction society was taking as the old Liberal establishment was breaking up. He foresaw the rise of a pluralistic society based on the emancipation of the popular masses of Calvinists, Catholics and Socialists; his political instincts were excellent.

But behind all these diverse characteristics and within this complex personality, there was a simple Christian heart. In his many meditations and even in newspaper articles and in speeches to the party faithful, this tender love for the Lord and concern for the salvation of souls was clearly visible. Behind the activist and the profound thinker was a remarkably transparent child of God. On many occasions Kuyper shared his deepest concern: to see men brought to Christ in order to live thankful and obedient lives before His face.

It is this great love for Christ the King and for integrated Christian service that makes Kuyper's witness of importance to all believers who call themselves Evangelical and Reformed. His witness was not an aberration and the stuff of folklore; it was a major act of witness to the cosmic implications of faith in Christ. Why God raised up Kuyper in such a small country is as much a mystery as the unique combination of his great vision and personal foibles.

B. Attitudes and Action

"Your life is to be one continuous flow of praise, one constant faithful service," wrote Kuyper in *The Practice of Godliness* (p. 88). This brief statement captures the relation between attitudes and action. The believer's attitude toward God and the world does determine the character of his action. Deep love for Christ issues forth as a comprehensive defense of the faith, a "cultural apologetic." There are two main parts to a comprehensive defense of the faith in modern secular culture: (1) an historical analysis of the problem of secularist modernity and (2) an articulation of an alternative comprehensive Christian perspective, often called a "Reformed worldview." A Christian's analysis of secular modernity reveals the existence of a basic religious antithesis between belief and unbelief and of the Christian's task over against the secular spirit. Groen's slogan summed up the first aspect: "the Gospel versus the Revolution." The second aspect of defending the faith in modern culture is the development of a Christian world-view based on an awareness of contemporary culture (the realm of common grace in which both man's sin and God's grace are at work) and the Christian church (the realm of special grace), and all of it under the Lordship of Christ. The episodes sketched in this book suggest the comprehensive character of Kuyper's cultural apologetic.

From this comprehensive apologetic flows a politically spiritual attitude towards public affairs and a strategy
for the reformation of culture. Political spirituality, the
ability to see both sin and grace in human affairs, gives
rise to a political strategy for social renewal. It must be
emphasized that Kuyper refused to reduce the Christian
faith to politics. Rather, he saw the profound implications of the Lordship of Christ over the common grace
realm of the nations as well as over the special grace realm
of the church. In national life he witnessed to the blessings of Christ which clash with human sin. The state is
God's instrument of common blessings to preserve
mankind for His higher purposes. Because of sin in the
world, believers must bring healing to state affairs as well
as take part in the affairs of the church. In the experience
of this statesman, perspective, program and performance
were united. He always tried to relate issues to the clash of
fundamental principles. Political spirituality, he knew, is
the application of sanctification to public affairs. Kuyper
chose the pluralist way of upholding Christian social
values in modern secular society, rejecting a theocratic
option as counter-productive and based on an improper
exegesis of Scripture.

In practical terms, Kuyper made the necessary connection between attitudes and action through public
media. He was a master at taking advantage of the
printed page and the speaker's podium. With printer's
ink in his blood, he made a sustained contribution to a
Christian newstask. A powerful public speaker, he could
hold a vast audience in the palm of his hand. By means of
a sustained media campaign, he was able to convince
hundreds of thousands of Reformed commoners of the
vital connection between political spirituality and Christian political action. His editorial voice kept tracing issues
back to the fundamental clash of principles. Kuyper was
able to educate his constituency in such a way that the
results are being felt generations later. For all of these
reasons, Kuyper's journalism and speeches are of lasting

value, even though the specific issues have long since faded. This principled media work sets Kuyper's accomplishments apart from the work of many other leaders of his day, both Christian and secular. But even journalism is not the whole story of success! In the way attitudes flowed into action during his lifetime, there remains something of Kuyper's personality and the mystery of God.

C. Kuyper's Position

One of the greatest strengths of this Christian statesman was his ability to articulate his position clearly. He related all the controversial issues of the day to certain basic principles to make visible the religious antithesis between truth and falsehood, devotion and idolatry, belief and unbelief, commitment and indifference. Piece by piece, his work painted the BIG PICTURE of the meaning of being a Christian in a secular world; tirelessly he constructed a comprehensive defence of the faith, a cultural apologetic. Some of the main ingredients of this comprehensive perspective follow: God is absolutely sovereign over all of creation. Jesus Christ is both the special-grace Head of the universal church and the common-grace Lord over the nations. The common blessings include the continuation of the seasons and the natural life processes, the restraining of the social effects of sin, and the endowment of people with certain gifts and abilities.

The concept of common grace allows one to develop an awareness of the great diversity within creation. We may speak of the structure of an apple, or of a mountain, the stars or the psychological make-up of the human mind. Many creational structures are related to the growth of human society such as the family, the state, private groups, education, the arts, politics, the media, and business. All of these structures ultimately point back to God's creative act. The Bible gives us the vantage point from which to discover the ordinances of God. This creational diversity, that which underlies the concept of "sphere sovereignty," impresses upon Christians the complexity of the ordinances of the Creator God and the interdependence of life. Aware of diversity, they recognize that the rights of the individual, of groups and of the state must be guaranteed.

The function of common grace is to enable society and all of creation to continue to carry out its God-ordained natural existence. The state, a divinely ordained institution, is an important agent of God's common grace. Human life and progress would be impossible without that common blessing, the state. Christian activity in culture presupposes that God is honored by our obedience to His common grace ordinances. Therefore it is possible for the preaching of the Gospel and the work of the church to accompany the quest for public justice and a meaningful life for all citizens.

Christ remains the special-grace Head of the church universal. He came into the world to die on the cross as an atonement for the sins of His people who respond to Him in repentance and faith. He was raised from the dead and He will return to claim His Bride and renew the cosmos. He has ordained the church to preach the Gospel, to teach and disciple the faithful. The common blessings, as they make human life possible, make possible the work of the church. Common grace and special grace are complimentary.

Another important aspect of the Kuyperian position is the distinction it draws between present and future aspects of the Kingdom of God. The Kingdom is present and growing but at the same time hidden. Only when Christ returns with power will it be completed. Even in the present situation, the Kingdom of God as it is manifested in the lives of Christians is broader than the institutional church. Believers may, then, fulfill their specific callings in culture, using their special talents, and do so in "Kingdom service." The cultural mandate to do all for God's glory must be carried out according to this wider perception of the Kingdom. Politics, education and scholarship, for example, are legitimate areas in which to work for God's glory and the healing which God's love brings.

Even though common blessings are visible and the Kingdom of God is active in the world, there remains a fundamental religious antithesis between belief and unbelief. This basic antithesis cuts through every aspect of life and is even at work in the life of each believer. This antithesis can also be observed in society in general and in politics in particular. The great struggle is always for or against the God who controls all things as the Radio Moscow commentator recognized on July 22, 1979.

Other important themes in Kuyper's thought: a Christian view of the state, the necessity for a viable pluralism of groups within society, and the quest for public justice. In a word, the state is the institution of God's common grace which retards the outworking of the social effects of sin and upholds public justice. As an agent of common grace, the state does not uphold any church creed nor impose civic punishment on heretics. Its task is to provide public justice for individuals and groups while allowing the full flowering of religious pluralism in informal and in institutional settings. It is in this context that Christians, as well as every other societal group, have the right to express their opinions and even to organize in order to influence national life. Christian action is not to be carried out by churches but by various types of Christian citizens' groups organized to deal with specific matters such as public policy, newscasting, research on Christian politics and controversial issues of the day.

D. The Kuyper Legacy for Today

Five main elements can be discerned in the legacy Kuyper has left for us. This legacy is not a blueprint for current action, but rather a starting point from which to develop a contemporary position. We may draw insight and inspiration from the perspective and the prac-

tice of Kuyper's historical experiment in political spirituality.

1. Comprehensive Gospel Witness. An integral part
of any contemporary expression of Christian political
stewardship must be a comprehensive Gospel witness.
The spiritual call for sinners to be converted to Christ and
then to live a consistent Christian life of stewardship must
be proclaimed. Salvation and sanctification go together.
God's people must realize that in their respective ways,
both the church and society need reformation. And
Christians engaged in the task of political renewal must
be given spiritual sustenance. The reality of spiritual conflict even in public affairs must be made clear. Politics is
never just politics; the deeper matters of life direction, of
worship, or idolatry, are always involved. Christians must
always attend to the full implications of the Gospel for
life, with special application to the public issues of the
day. The lines between belief and unbelief must be drawn
clearly. Justice must be contrasted to injustice. Truth in
newscasting must be distinguished from falsehood.
Religious currents in national and international life must
be examined. In sum, Christians must demonstrate the
full relevance of the Gospel, starting with biblical in-
fallibility, the new birth, and the reality of spiritual encouragement in the Christian faith.

2. The Kingship of Christ and Common Grace. In
order for any Christian political expression to be viable on
a long-term basis, it must clearly affirm the Lordship of
Christ over the nations. The Second Coming overshadows
all of our political work, for we know that He will come to
judge the nations as well as individuals. Since God, the
Lord of history, is in ultimate control of the world, we can
never have a totally pessimistic outlook on life. He may
have surprises for us. Furthermore, the reality of common

grace and the promise given to Noah after the flood that the natural order would continue until the end of time give us the encouragement that our work in the world is not in vain. Christian activity in common areas of human life brings healing and prepares the way for the outworking of the Gospel. Christian attention to such important problems as world hunger, international tensions and the increasing abortion rate is vitally important, for it demonstrates that the Christian doctrine that man is created in God's image is of great importance to the survival of all men. Serving Christ in the diverse areas of life, including politics, is not a rejection of duty. Such service reflects the Christian understanding of the quality of life experienced in part by men in general and culminating in the new life in Christ. Both the Kingship of Christ and common grace give us a sense of balanced realism in our approach to public affairs; we are equipped to see both the sin of man and the grace of God.

3. The Historical Sense of the Christian Task. There must be serious prayer, Bible study and reflection concerning the flow of events before believers can discern their individual and collective tasks in a secular society. The problem is not that Western society is openly atheistic but rather that it is religiously indifferent to the Christian faith. Because of the subtle ways a secular society ignores God, many believers are unaware of the scope and power of the attacks made on the residue of a Christian heritage in society and on the Gospel itself. Usually these attacks seem innocuous and even glamorous: personal preference becomes the highest norm for life while secular humanism glorifies autonomy and the power of modern man. However, what is being attacked, ultimately, is the biblical view of reality: man's fall into sin, his need of a savior, Christ's atoning death for His people, His rule over the universe and His triumphant coming again.

Believers must be aware of how secularism has risen to cultural dominance in the Western world since the eighteenth century. At the same time they must realize that the Reformation was a movement of spiritual renewal in church and culture which has deeply influenced countries such as Great Britain, Holland, Germany, the United States and Canada. There is a definite historical antithesis between the unfolding humanism of the Enlightenment and the French Revolution on the one hand, and the unfolding renewal of Christian faith and action of the Reformation tradition on the other. It is in the context of this historical antithesis that we must see our own response to the cultural mandate in public affairs. We must be willing to profit from the experience and insight of Christians in past ages who have struggled with such problems as the meaning of secularity, poverty, propaganda, injustice, social conflict, and democratic reformism. We must not think that ours is the first generation of believers to struggle with these problems. In this regard the experience and insight of the Christian Democratic tradition in general and of Kuyper's Anti-Revolutionary Party in particular can aid our reflection a great deal. Any group of Christians with politically spiritual intentions must engage in historical reflection as well as study current problems. With a sense of their strategic place in history, Christians can more effectively decide how to set priorities and how to best use their talents.

In every situation Christians must make a fundamental break with all forms of political humanism (conservatism, centrism, liberalism and Marxism) in order to articulate a contemporary Christian Democratic option. Such an option seeks to develop its own perspective and agenda based on the total Lordship of Christ. A genuine break with humanism entails a comprehensive reformation of thought and attitudes, using the best insights reformational scholarship can provide for history, philosophy, theology and political science. Determining the outlines of a distinctively Christian Democratic or politically spiritual option requires historical research and serious reflection on the current situation. Kuyper's example is especially instructive in this regard.

We must also rule out as a basis for Christian action an ecumenical synthesis between those who believe in the scriptural Gospel and those who accept only a vague notion of Christendom. It would be counter-productive to reject one form of a synthesis with humanism (such as conservatism or Marxism) while accepting another. Yet on the level of practical cooperation in order to deal with certain clearly defined issues, a policy of limited cobelligerency may be possible. Fundamental Christian principles and commitment to the Gospel should not be compromised, however. Kuyper's defense of this position merits our serious consideration.

4. Comprehensive and Comprehensible Media Work. An essential ingredient for Christian renewal in society is sustained and intelligent media communications. Radio, TV, newsprint, cassettes, books, and publications of all kinds must be used to communicate the implications of belief in the Lord Christ. And Christian newscasting should be a priority. In local, national, and world newscasting, the antithesis between truth and disinformation becomes clear. My perception of this antithesis has been sharpened by my own years of listening to regular short-wave broadcasts from stations such as Radio Moscow, the BBC (London), Radio Israel, Radio Peking, Radio Havana, Radio Canada International, and Radio Australia.

A politically spiritual perspective must be given clearly and on a regular basis in the media. A world-view perspective cannot be built overnight, but serious news reporting which constantly attempts to relate issues to principles could do much to educate people and to set priorities for action. Moreover, a Christian newstask in itself is a legitimate aspect of stewardship. Any such media efforts will have to be based on the foundations of Reformed scholarship. The goal of comprehensive and comprehensible media work will not be realized tomorrow, but first steps must be taken. For it is the media which teaches people what current truth and acceptable attitudes are. Since the secular media preaches an attractive humanistic set of values, believers should undertake their own media effort which witnesses to Christian values.

5. *Political Spirituality, Justice and the Rights of Groups.* From the experience of Abraham Kuyper it is possible to conclude that those with a politically spiritual perspective may be given the opportunity to influence public opinion or public policy. Political spirituality is an attitude that calls for action. Political power is not to be feared by those called of God to be statesmen. This attitude is not an ivory tower theory; it emerged from active involvement in public affairs. Political spirituality can and should motivate a quest for public justice. It is sometimes difficult to decide on a just course of action, for complicated issues are often involved. Nevertheless, the central task of the state is to bear the sword of justice. As Christians carry out their stewardship in public affairs, they must struggle to relate their perspective to the rights of groups and individuals, locally, nationally, and globally.

If God should bring Christian statesmen into important leadership or advisory positions, the experience and insight of the Kuyperian tradition could help give them a sense of direction and priorities for attention. But even if no Christian political leaders appear, the articulation of a politically spiritual position can be a powerful witness to the total claims of Christ. It is for this latter reason that the historian presents to the public the insights and experience of the Christian Democratic tradition. Abraham

Kuyper's practice of political spirituality represents a high point of the attempt to forge a Christian Democratic alternative to all forms of humanist politics including liberalism, conservatism, socialism and Marxism. "Therefore in the affairs of the nation, as well as in all other spheres of life," wrote this great man in *The Practice of Godliness*, "the Christian is called upon to fight the fight of faith, to be a soldier of Jesus Christ. If we fail to obey the command of God, if we fail to defend the right, we shall suffer the downfall of the church and of the nation" (p. 42).

Bibliographical Note

REFERENCE IS MADE HERE TO the main primary and secondary sources used in this book. Since virtually all of this material is in foreign-language sources, footnotes have been eliminated. Interested scholars can consult the sources referred to below. A list for further reading has been included for those who wish to study aspects of matters referred to in this book.

1. Primary Sources

Daily Newspaper: *De Standaard*, 1872-1874, 1879, 1908, 1914 (Amsterdam). Volumes of speeches: K. Groen, ed. *Geen Vergeefs Woord: Verzamelde Deputaten-Redevoeringen*, Kampen, J.H. Kok, 1951; A. Kuyper *Parlementaire Redevoeringen*, Amsterdam, Van Holkema & Warendorf, for the years 1895-1904, 3 vols.; R.C. Verweijck, ed., *Dr. A. Kuyper in Jezus Ontslapen*, Baarn, E.J. Bosch, 1920.

Other writings by Kuyper: *Confidentie*, Amsterdam, Hoveker, 1873; *Souvereiniteit in Eigen Kring* (1880), Kampen, J.H. Kok, 1930; *Christianity and the Class Struggle* (1891), trans. Dirk Jellema, Grand Rapids, Piet Hein, 1950; *De Gemeene Gratie*, Kampen, J.H. Kok, 1903-1904, 3 vols.; *Pro Rege of het Koningschap van Christus*, Kampen, J.H. Kok, 1911-1912, 3 vols.; *Anti-Revolutionaire Staatkunde*, Kampen, J.H. Kok, 1911-1912, 2 vols.; *The Practice of Godliness*, trans. Marian Schooland, Grand Rapids, Baker, 1948, 1977; *De Overheid: Locus de Magistratu*, Kampen, J.H. Kok, no year.

The writings of Groen van Prinsterer: *Briefwisseling, 1866-1876*, A. Goslinga & J.L. van Essen, eds., The Hague, Martinus Nijhoff, vol.

IV; *Ongeloof en Revolutie* (1847, 1868), H. Smitskamp, ed., Franeker, T. Wever, 1951; *Unbelief and Revolution*, trans. and ed. by Harry Van Dyke with Donald Morton, Amsterdam, Groen van Prinsterer Fund, 1973, 1976, 2 vols.

2. Secondary Sources

P.A. Diepenhorst, *Dr. A. Kuyper*, Haarlem, De Erven F. Bohn, 1931; P. Kasteel, *Abraham Kuyper*, Kampen, J.H. Kok, 1938; P.J. Oud, *Honderd Jaar: Een Eeuw van Staatkundige Vormgeving in Nederland, 1840-1940*, Assen, Van Gorcum; G. Puchinger, *Gesprek over de Onbekende Kuyper*, Kampen, J.H. Kok, 1971; G. Puchinger, *Ontmoetingen met Anti-Revolutionairen*, Zutphen, Terra, 1981; G.J. Schutte, *Mr. Groen van Prinsterer*, Goes, Ooosterbaan & Le Cointre, 1976; C. Smeenk and J.A. De Wilde, *Het Volk ten Baat: De Geschiedenis van de AR-Partij*, Groningen, Jan Haan; 1949; Frank VandenBerg, *Abraham Kuyper* (1960), St. Catharines, Ontario, Paideia Press, 1978.

3. Further Reading

A number of issues raised in this book can be studied with help from works published mostly in English. Much historical research and evaluation remains to be done on Kuyper, on the Anti-Revolutionary political tradition, and on the larger context of the European Christian Democratic (Catholic) parties, as well as the wider currents of the Evangelical revival movement begun in Europe in the nineteenth century.

Konrad Adenauer, *Memoires, 1945-53*, trans. Beate Ruhm von Oppen, Chicago, Henry Regnery, 1966.
C. Den Hollander, ed., *Christian Political Options*, The Hague, Anti-Revolutionary Party, 1979.
Michael Fogarty, *Christian Democracy in Western Europe, 1820-1953*, Westport, Conn., Greenwood, 1957, 1974.
Bob Goudzwaard, *A Christian Political Option*, Toronto, Wedge, 1972.
Ronald E.M. Irving, *Christian Democracy in France*, London, George Allen & Unwin, 1973.
——— *The Christian Democratic Parties of Western Europe*, London, Royal Institute for International Affairs and George Allen & Unwin, 1979.
Elizabeth Kluit, *Het Protestantse Reveil in Nederland en Daarbuiten, 1815-1865*, Amsterdam, J.H. Paris, 1970.
Abraham Kuyper, *Christianity as a Life-System*, Memphis, Christian Studies Center, 1980 (abridgement of *Lectures on Calvinism*,

Grand Rapids, William B. Eerdmans, 1931, 1961).

McKendree R. Langley, "Gospel and Party: Notes on the History of the Anti-Revolutionary Party in The Netherlands" (unpublished class syllabus, 1978).

——— "The Political Spirituality of Abraham Kuyper" *International Reformed Bulletin*, no. 76, 1979.

——— "The Witness of a World View," *Pro Rege*, December, 1979 (on Groen van Prinsterer).

——— "God and Liberty: The Catholic Quest for Democratic Pluralism from Lamennais to Vatican II," *Pro Rege*, June, 1980.

——— "Creation and Sphere Sovereignty in Historical Perspective," *Pro Rege*, June, 1981.

——— "Robert Schuman and the Politics of Reconciliation," *Pro Rege*, June, 1982.

Richard Lovelace, *Dynamics of Spiritual Life: An Evangelical Theology of Renewal*, Downer's Grove, Ill., Inter-Varsity, 1979.

J. Gresham Machen, "Christianity and Culture," *Princeton Theological Review*, January, 1913.

——— "Faith and History," *Princeton Theological Review*, July, 1915.

——— *Christianity and Liberalism*, Grand Rapids, Eerdmans, no year.

Francis A. Schaeffer, *The Church at the End of the Twentieth Century*, Downers Grove, Ill., Inter-Varsity, 1970.

——— *True Spirituality*, Wheaton, Ill., Tyndale House, 1971.

Robert Schuman, *Pour l'Europe*, Paris, Nagel, 1964.

James Skillen, *Christians Organizing for Political Service*, Washington, D.C., Association for Public Justice, 1980.

J.M. Spier, *Introduction to Christian Philosophy*, trans. David H. Freeman, Philadelphia, Presbyterian and Reformed, 1954.

Gordon Spykman et al., *State, Society and Schools: A Case for Structural and Confessional Pluralism*, Grand Rapids, William B. Eerdmans, 1981.

Cornelius Van Til, *Defense of the Faith*, Philadelphia, Presbyterian and Reformed, 1955.

Henry R. Van Til, *The Calvinistic Concept of Culture*, Philadelphia, Presbyterian and Reformed, 1959.

Geerhardus Vos, *The Preaching of Jesus Concerning the Kingdom of God and the Church*, Philadelphia, Presbyterian and Reformed, 1972.

S.U. Zuidema, "Common Grace and Christian Action in Abraham Kuyper" in *Confrontation and Communication*, Toronto, Wedge, 1972.